CONTENTS

 W9-ADT-442

Consonants

UNIT 1 — Theme: Family and Friends

Short Vowels

UNIT 2 — Theme: Amazing Animals

6 7 8 9 10 DP 05 04 03 02 01 00 99

Long Vowels
UNIT 3
Theme: Let's Play

Consonant Blends, Y as a Vowel
UNIT 4
Theme: Everybody Eats

Endings, Digraphs, Contractions
UNIT 5
Theme: Whatever the Weather

Read Along

WISHING WELL LETTERS

Wishing well,
Wishing well,
Share some letters,
Sounds to tell.

Call your family,
Call your friends.
Sharing stories,
Without end.

▶ How many letters can you find?

THINK! What wish would you make at this wishing well?

Home Letter

Dear Family,

In the next few weeks we will be learning about consonants. We will review the names of the consonants and how to print the letters. We will also learn many words that begin and end with consonant sounds.

Ben   Dad   Mom   Kit   Tip

Many names of family members and friends begin and end with consonants. In this unit, we will also learn about what it means to be part of a family and to have friends.

At-Home Activities

Here are some activities you and your child might like to do together.

▶ Ask your child to draw a picture of your family. Help him or her print the names of family members under their pictures. Point to different consonant letters in each name. Ask your child to identify the letters.

▶ Help your child make a Letter Book that can be added to from time to time. Your child can print a letter on each page, then tape or paste pictures that begin with that letter.

Book Corner

You and your child might enjoy reading these books together.

The Relatives Came
by Cynthia Rylant
Everyone has a delightful time when relatives from Virginia come to visit.

May'naise Sandwiches & Sunshine Tea
by Sandra Belton
This story is about the importance of family and family history.

Sincerely,

Bb go together.
Bb are partner letters.

▶ **Color** each ball that has partner letters on it.

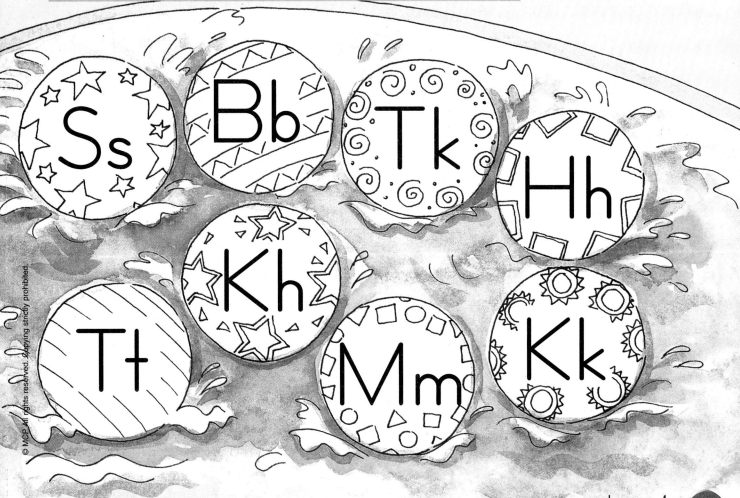

1

S

card
sail
sun
meat
sock

2

b

Beth
Sam
Ben
Bonnie
Mona

3

H

home
boat
hill
king
hook

4

k

Ken
Karen
Tammy
Kurt
Matt

5

M

nose
monkey
hand
milk
mask

6

t

Tom
Tony
Tina
Lila
Marco

7

B

dish
boys
bug
top
bowl

8

s

Steve
Sarah
Bobby
Katie
Sue

9

m

Mike
Helen
May
Henry
Kim

Suzy sat on the sand.
Suzy sat by the sea.
Suzy sat in the sun.
Suzy sat with me.

▶ Sand **begins with the sound of s.** Circle
each picture whose name begins with **s.**

1

2

3

4

5

6

7

8

9

10

11

12

1

Ss

2

3

4

5

6

7

8

9

10

11

12

 Home

Say the name of each picture. Ask your child to clap if the word begins with the sound of *s.*

Teddy Bear, Teddy Bear,
Tap your nose.
Teddy Bear, Teddy Bear,
Tap your toes.

Toes begins with the sound of **t**. Circle each picture whose name begins with the sound of **t**.

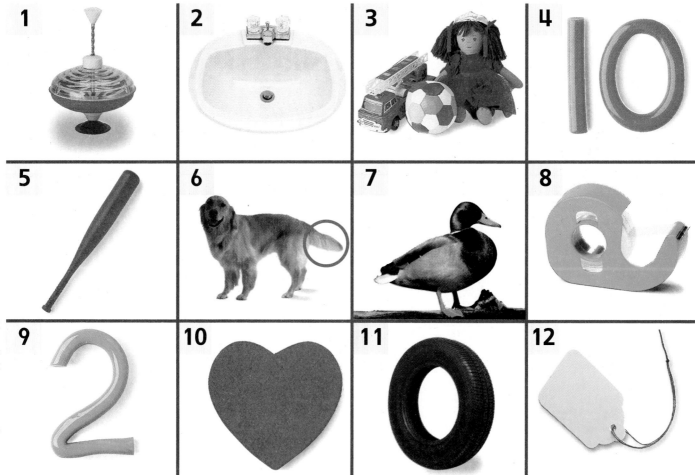

1	2	3	4
5	6	7	8
9	10	11	12

Say the name of each picture. If it begins with the sound of **t**, print **Tt** on the line.

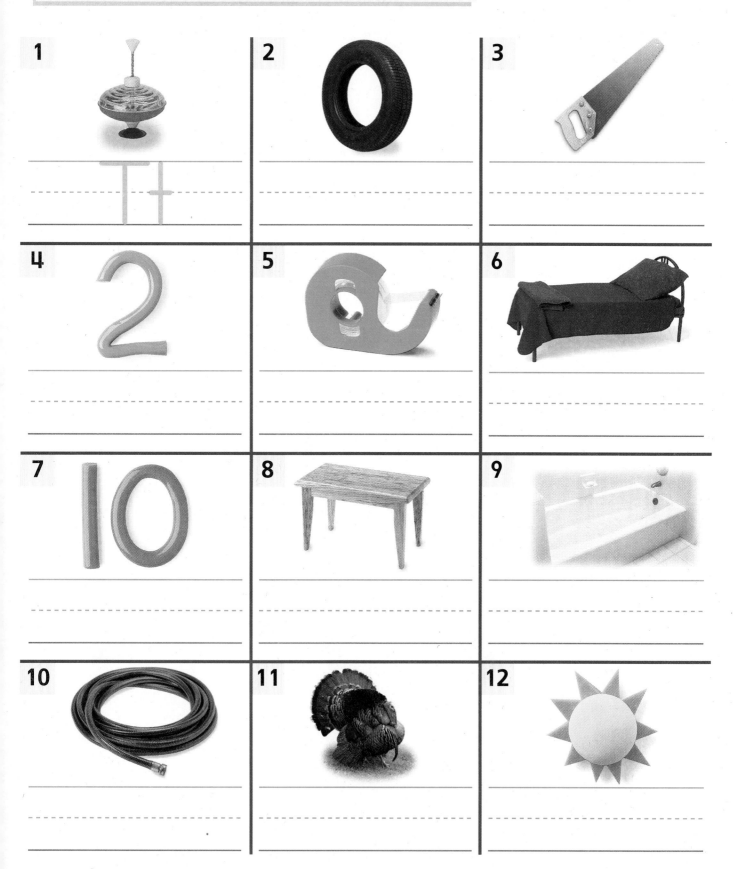

1 Tt

2

3

4

5

6

7

8

9

10

11

12

10 Lesson 3
The sound of t

Ask your child to name three objects in your home that begin with the sound of *t*.

Let's bounce the ball high,
Let's bounce the ball low.
Let's bounce the ball fast,
Let's bounce the ball slow.

▶ **Ball** begins with the sound of **b**. **Circle** each picture whose name begins with the sound of **b**.

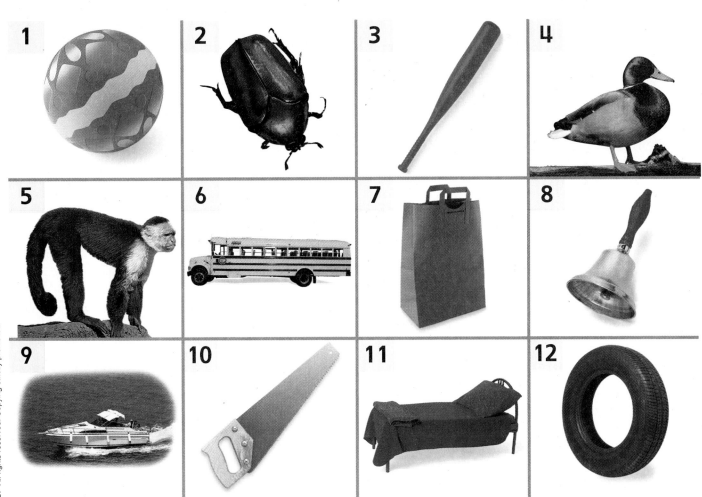

1
2
3
4
5
6
7
8
9
10
11
12

Lesson 4
The sound of b: Phonemic awareness

11

Say the name of each picture. If it begins with the sound of **b**, print **Bb** on the line.

1

Bb

2

3

4

5

6

7

8

9

10

11

12

Lesson 4
The sound of b

Home

Say "Buddy bought a ___." Ask your child to add a word that begins with the sound of b.

Say the name of each picture. If the name begins with the sound of the letter in the box, **print** it on the first line. If it ends with that sound, **print** it on the second line.

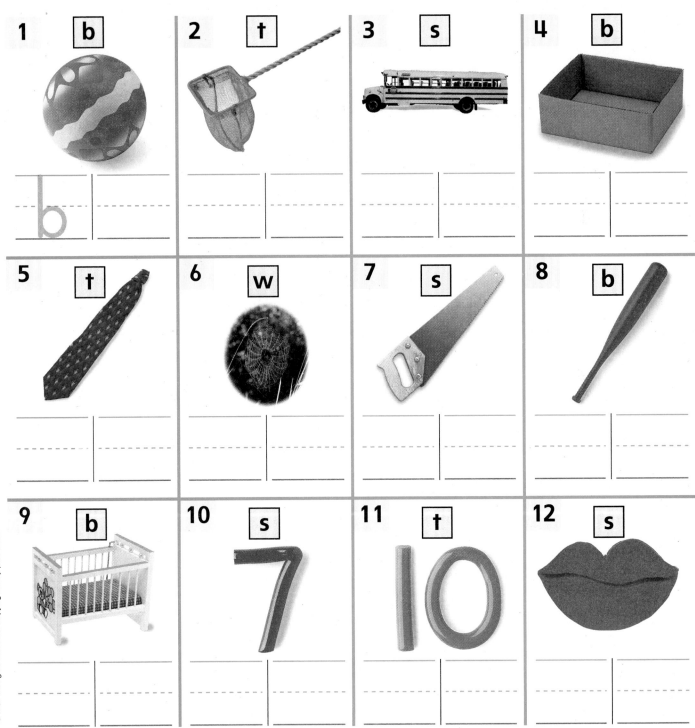

Say each picture name. Draw a line through the pictures in a row that begin with the same letter sound. Write the letter that wins in each game.

1.

2.

3.

Lesson 5
Review consonants s, t, b

Home

Ask your child to name the pictures in the winning row of each game board.

Hop, hop, hop!
Hop in a row.
Hop, hop, hop!
Hop high and low.

► **Hop** begins with the sound of **h**. Say the name of each picture. Circle the beginning letter of the picture name. Then circle each picture whose name begins with the sound of **h**.

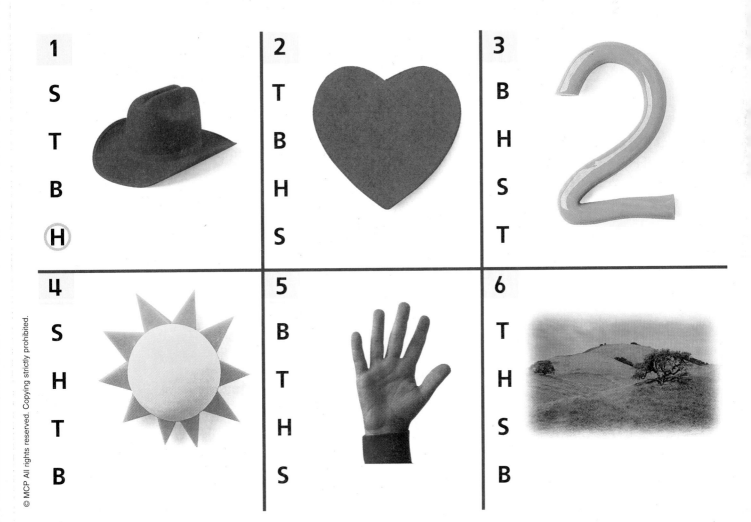

1
S
T
B
(H)

2
T
B
H
S

3
B
H
S
T

4
S
H
T
B

5
B
T
H
S

6
T
H
S
B

Say the name of each picture. If it begins with the sound of h, print Hh on the line.

1 
Hh

2

3

4

5

6

7

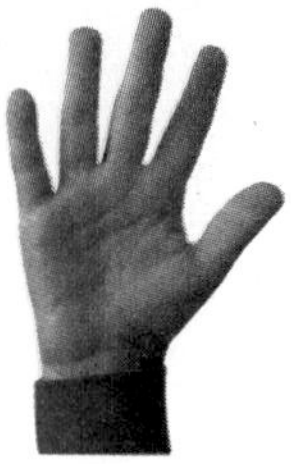

8

9

10

11

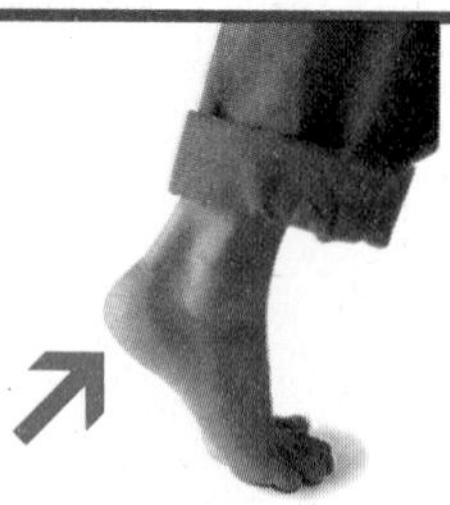

12

Lesson 6
The sound of h

Name a picture. Ask your child whether or not the word begins with the sound of h.

Mom gave me a muffin for lunch.
Mom gave me a muffin to munch.
The muffin I munched was yummy.
The muffin is in my tummy.

Mom begins with the sound of **m**. Circle each picture whose name begins with the sound of **m**.

1

2

3

4

5

6

7

8

9

10

11

12

Say the name of each picture. If it begins with the sound of **m**, print **Mm** on the line.

1	2	3
Mm		

4	5	6

7	8	9

10	11	12

Lesson 7
The sound of m

Home

Point to a picture. Have your child say its name and then repeat the sound at the beginning of the word.

Where's Katy's kite?
Where's Katy's key?
Where's Katy's kitty?
Katy has lost all three!

▶ **Kite** begins with the sound of **k**. Say the name of each picture. Circle the beginning letter of the picture name. Then circle each picture whose name begins with the sound of **k**.

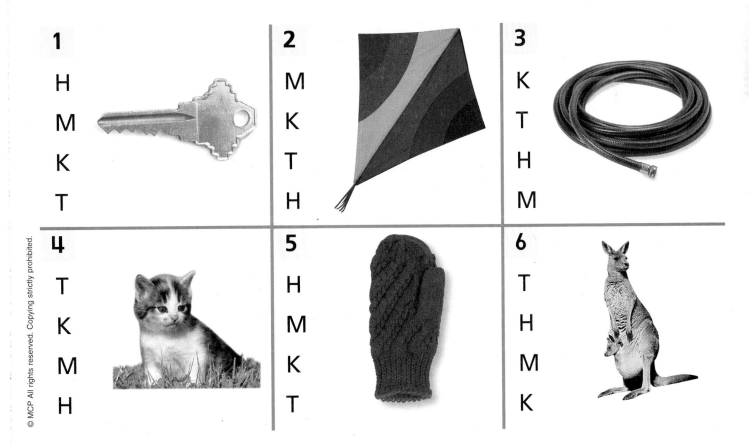

1
H
M
K
T

2
M
K
T
H

3
K
T
H
M

4
T
K
M
H

5
H
M
K
T

6
T
H
M
K

Say the name of each picture. If it begins with the sound of **k**, print **Kk** on the line.

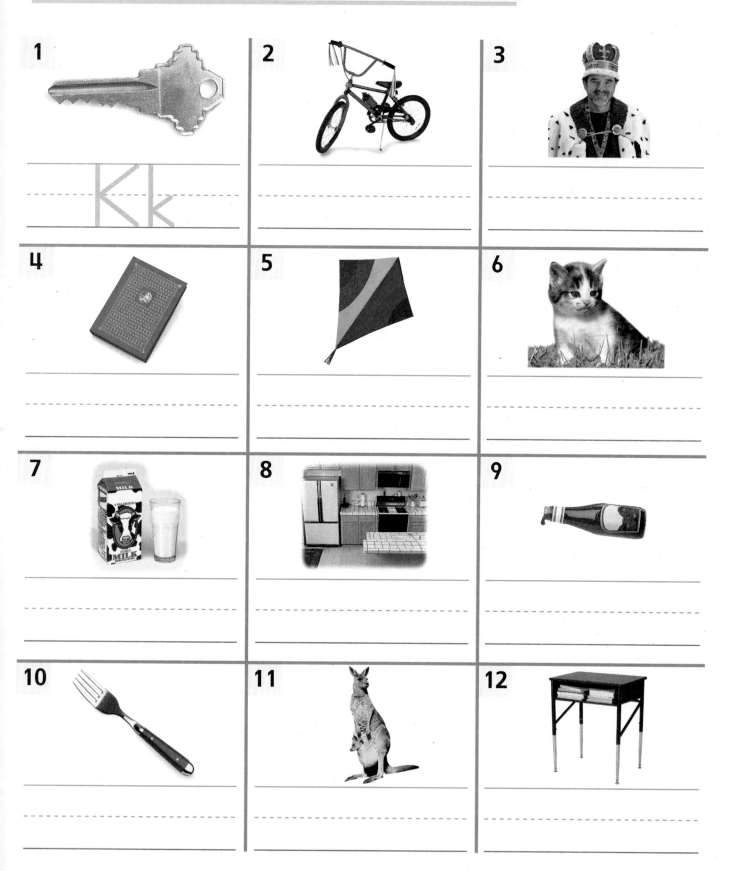

1

Kk

2

3

4

5

6

7

8

9

10

11

12

Lesson 8
The sound of k

 Home

Take turns with your child, naming pictures that begin with the sound of *k*.

Say the name of each picture. Find the beginning letter of each picture name. **Circle** that letter.

1	**2**	**3**
H M K	M K H	K H M
4	**5**	**6**
H M K	K M H	M H K
7	**8**	**9**
H K M	K M H	M H K
10	**11**	**12**
H K M	K M H	M H K

Lesson 9
Review: Consonants h, m, k

21

Say the name of each picture. If the name begins with the sound of the letter in the box, **print** it on the first line. If it ends with that sound, **print** it on the second line.

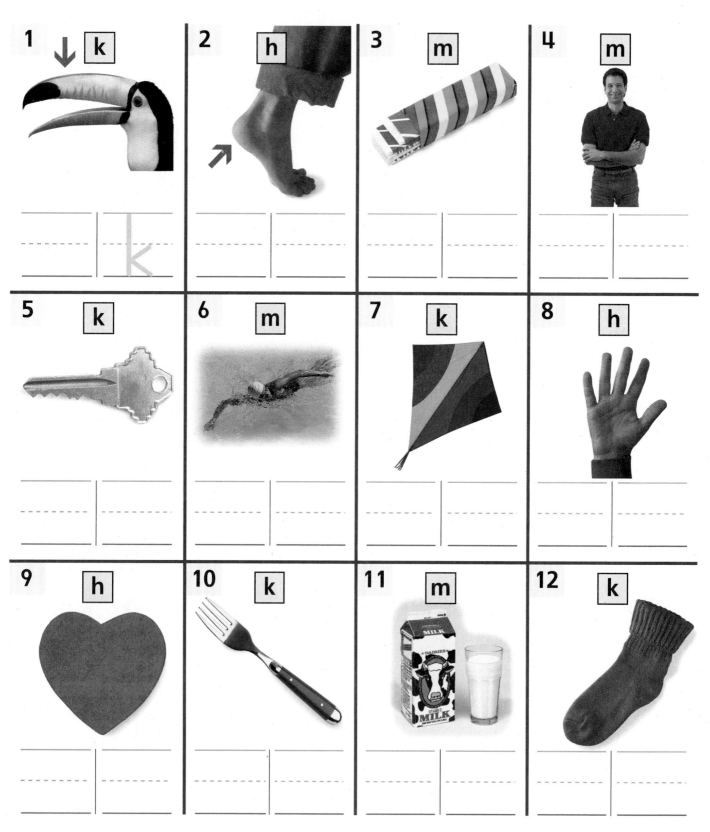

1. ↓ k

2. h ↗

3. m

4. m

5. k

6. m

7. k

8. h

9. h

10. k

11. m

12. k

Lesson 9
Review: Consonants h, m, k

Home

Ask your child to name two pictures that begin and two that end with the same sound.

Say the name of each picture. Print the letter
for its beginning sound on the first line. Then print
the letter for its ending sound on the second line.

1 b s	**2**	**3**
4	**5**	**6**
7	**8**	**9**
10	**11**	**12**

Read the words in the box. **Print** letters in the boxes to make words that will name each picture.

bus
book
hat
hook
man
tub

1. a

2.

3.

4. o   o
o

5. u

6.

Lesson 10
Review consonants s, t, b, h, m, k

Home

Ask your child which words in the box rhyme.

Dd go together.
Dd are partner letters.

Color each duck that has partner letters on it.

Partner letters Jj, Ff, Gg, Ll, Dd, Nn

▶ **Circle the partner letters in each box.**

1 g j D G	**2** F f d L	**3** N l n M
4 g T J j	**5** K l L f	**6** d B g D
7 j C G g	**8** l f F H	**9** h F n N
10 j g S J	**11** D d b g	**12** t L D l

Lesson 11
Partner letters: Jj, Ff, Gg, Ll, Dd, Nn

Home

Print a capital letter from the page. Have your child print the matching small letter.

J my name is Janie.
My brother's name is Jack.
We jump forward
And then jump back.

▶ **Jump** begins with the sound of **j**. **Circle** each picture whose name begins with the sound of **j**.

1	**2**	**3**
4	**5**	**6**
7	**8**	**9**

1

2

3

4

5

6

7

8

9

10

11

12

Home

Ask your child to say the names of all the pictures that begin with the sound of *j*.

Five furry foxes
Fanning in the heat.
They all run away
On furry fox feet.

▶ **Five** begins with the sound of **f.** Circle each picture whose name begins with the sound of **f.**

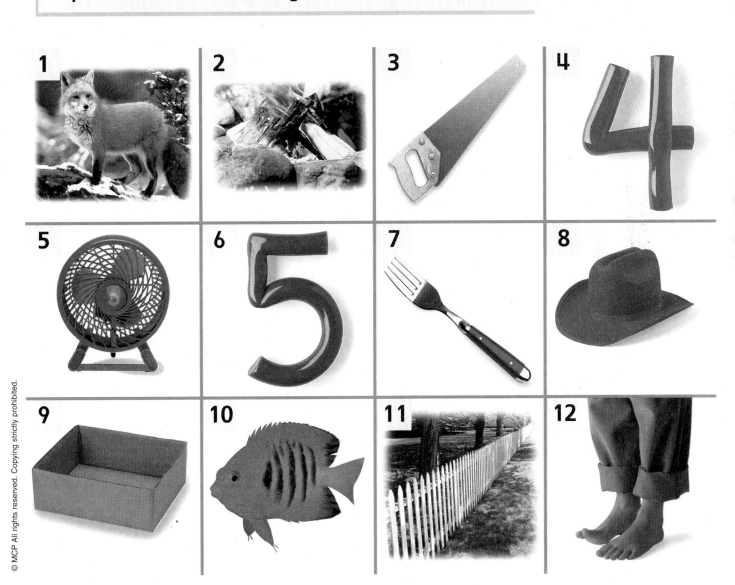

Say the name of each picture. If it begins with the sound of **f**, print **Ff** on the line.

1	**2**	**3**
Ff		
4	**5**	**6**
7	**8**	**9**
10	**11**	**12**

Lesson 13
The sound of f

 Home

Ask your child to name four pictures whose names begin with the sound of **f**.

The good little goose
Said to the goat,
"If you give me grapes,
I'll give you some oats."

▶ **Good** begins with the sound of **g**. Circle each picture whose name begins with the sound of **g**.

1

2

3

4

5

6

7

8

9

Say the name of each picture. If it begins with the sound of g, print Gg on the line.

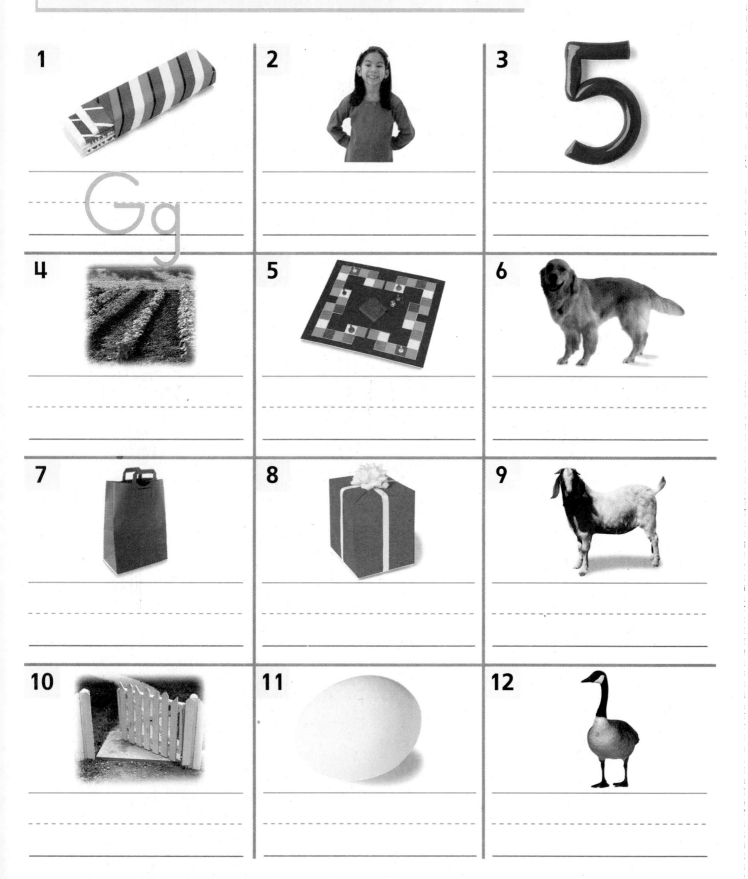

1

Gg

2

3

4

5

6

7

8

9

10

11

12

Lesson 14
The sound of g

Home

Take turns with your child, naming
pictures that begin with the sound of g.

> **Say** the name of each picture. If the name begins with the sound of the letter in the box, **print** it on the first line. If it ends with that sound, **print** it on the second line.

1. f

2. j

3. g

4. f

5. g

6. f

7. f

8. j

9. g

10. j

11. g

12. f

Say the name of each toy. **Write** a letter to finish the word on each sign. Then **trace** the word.

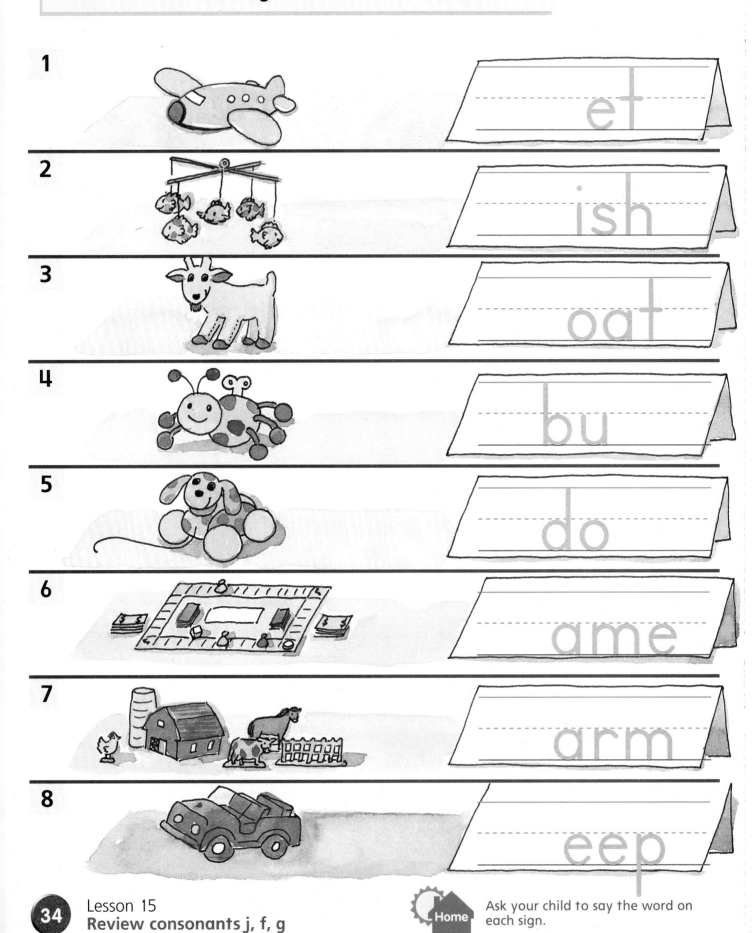

1   et

2   ish

3   oat

4   bu

5   do

6   ame

7   arm

8   eep

Lesson 15
Review consonants j, f, g

Home

Ask your child to say the word on each sign.

Lick, lick the lollipops.
Will they last long?
Lick, lick the lollipops.
They're almost gone!

Lick begins with the sound of l. Circle each picture whose name begins with l.

1 	**2** 	**3** 	**4** 
5 	**6** 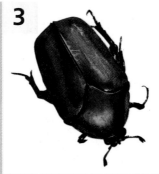	**7** 	**8** 
9 	**10** 	**11** 	**12** 

Say the name of each picture. If it begins with the sound of l, print Ll on the line.

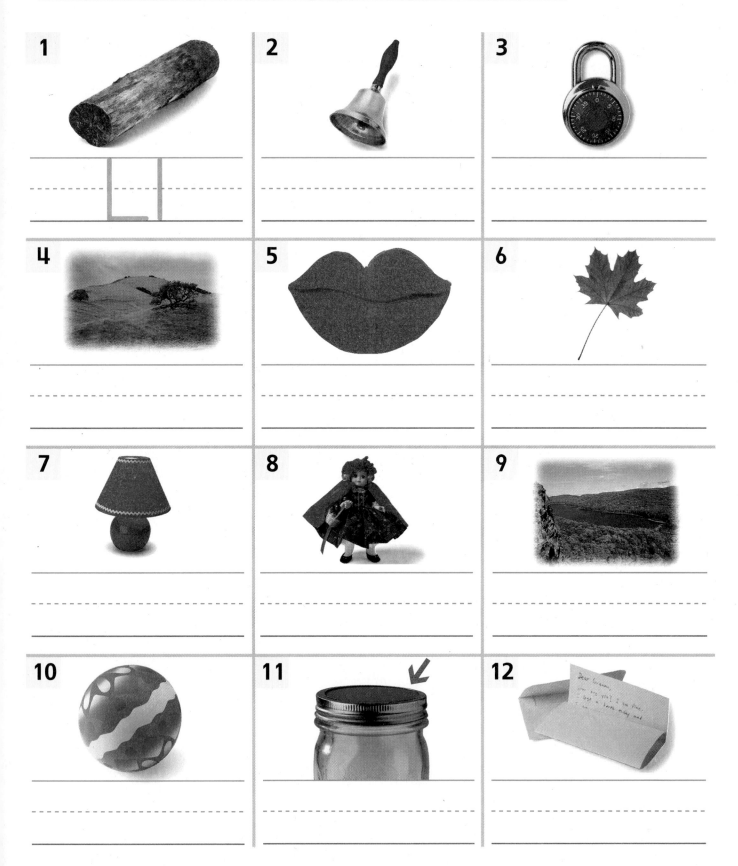

1

2

3

4

5

6

7

8

9

10

11

12

Lesson 16
The sound of l

Home

Ask your child to name three pictures whose names begin with the sound of *l*.

Denny does the dishes.
Dorie does them, too.
Dad feeds the dog,
And soon they are through.

► Dishes **begins with the sound of d. Circle** each picture whose name begins with the sound of **d**.

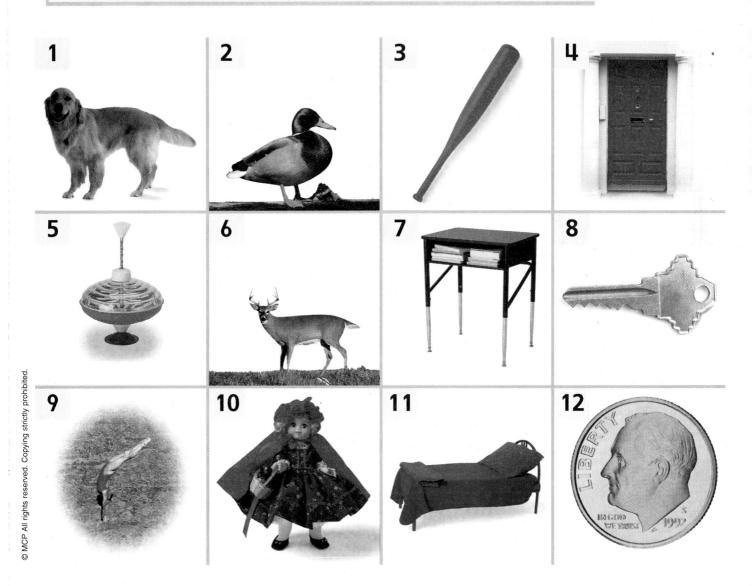

1	2	3	4
5	6	7	8
9	10	11	12

Say the name of each picture. If it begins with the sound of **d**, print **Dd** on the line.

1 Dd	**2**	**3**
4	**5**	**6**
7	**8**	**9**
10	**11**	**12**

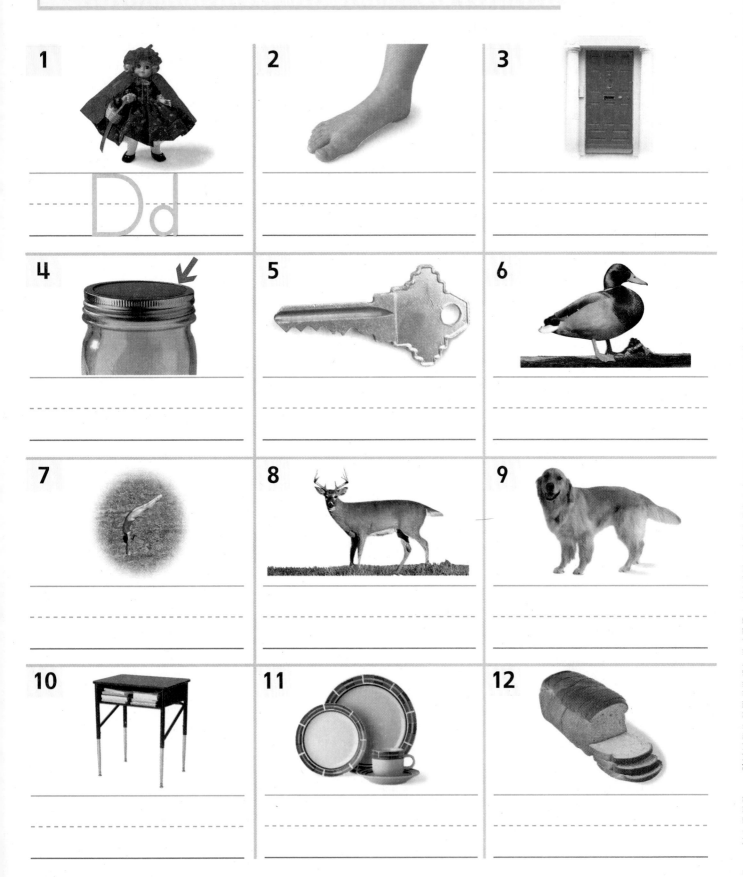

Lesson 17
The sound of d

 Home

Ask your child to name three objects in your home that begin with the *d* sound.

No, no, Nellie.
No, no, Ned.
Do not jump up
On my nice neat bed.

▶ **No** begins with the sound of **n**. Circle each picture whose name begins with the sound of **n**.

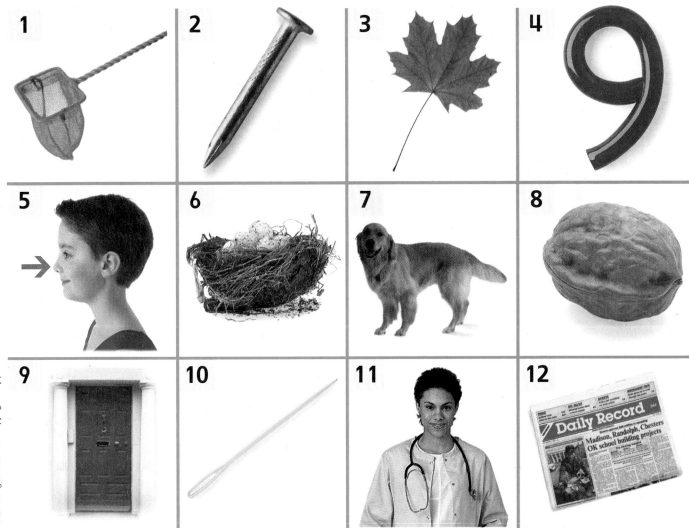

1	2	3	4
5 →	6	7	8
9	10	11	12

Say the name of each picture. If it begins with the sound of **n**, print **Nn** on the line.

1
Nn

2

3

4

5

6

7

8

9

10

11

12

Lesson 18
The sound of n

 Home

Say the name of each picture. Ask your child to clap if the word begins with the sound of *n*.

Say the name of each picture. If the name begins with the sound of the letter in the box, print it on the first line. If it ends with that sound, print it on the second line.

1	n	2	l	3	d	4	n

n

5	d	6	l	7	n	8	d

9	n	10	l	11	d	12	l

Lesson 19
Review consonants l, d, n

41

Say the name of the little pictures in the boxes. **Look** for these pictures in the big picture. **Circle** each picture you find. **Write** the letter of each beginning sound.

1

2

3

4

5

6

Lesson 19
Review consonants l, d, n

Say: I am furry and have four legs. "**What am I?**" Ask your child to solve the riddle with a picture name.

Say the name of each picture. Print the letter for its beginning sound on the first line. Then print the letter for its ending sound on the second line.

1	2	3	4
b t			

5	6	7	8

9	10	11	12

Say the name of each picture. Print the letter for its beginning sound on the first line. Then print the letter for its ending sound on the second line.

1

s | n

2

3

4

5

6

7

8

9

10

11

12

Lesson 20
Review s, t, b, h, m, k, j, f, g, l, d, n

Home

Ask your child to tell what letters stand for the beginning and ending sounds of a picture.

Look at the first letter in the row. **Color** each picture that has the partner letter on it.

1

P

r	p	q	p
p	j	p	c

2

W

V	w	w	M
m	w	v	w

3

R

Q	r	P	r
r	v	q	r

Lesson 21
Partner letters Ww, Cc, Rr, Pp, Qq, Vv

45

Find the two sets of partner letters in each box.
Color the shapes for one set of partner letters red.
Color the shapes for the other set blue.

1.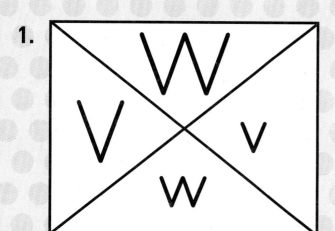

2.

3.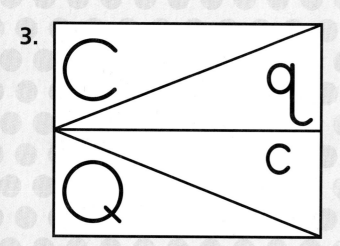

4.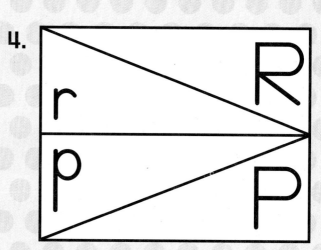

5.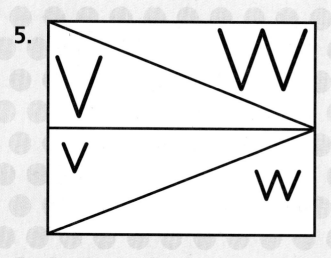

6.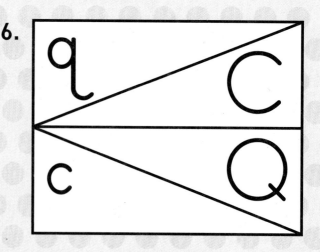

Lesson 21
Partner letters: Ww, Cc, Rr, Pp, Qq, Vv

 Home

Print a capital letter from the page.
Have your child print the matching
small letter.

We watch from the window
As winter winds blow.
We watch from the window,
And wish it would snow.

► **Window** begins with the sound of **w**. Circle each picture whose name begins with the sound of **w**.

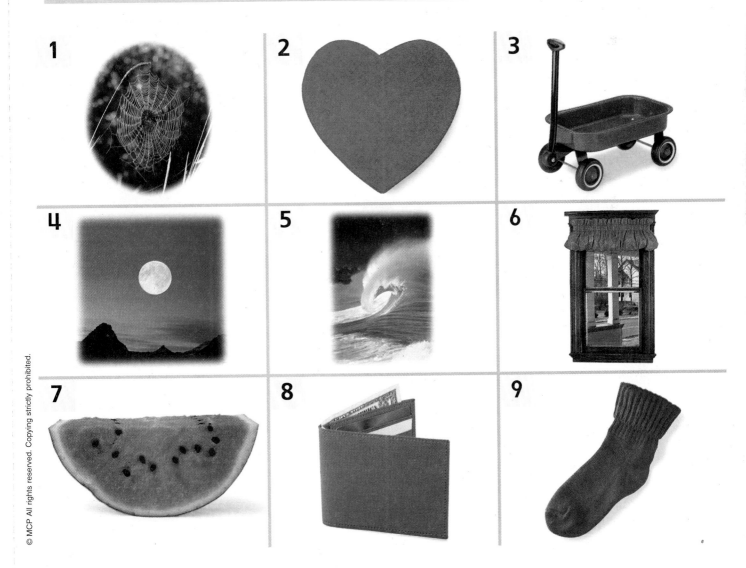

1

2

3

4

5

6

7

8

9

Say the name of each picture. If it begins with the sound of **w**, print **Ww** on the line.

1

Ww

2

3

4

5

6

7

8

9

10

11

12

Lesson 22
The sound of w

Ask your child to name three pictures whose names begin with the sound of *w*.

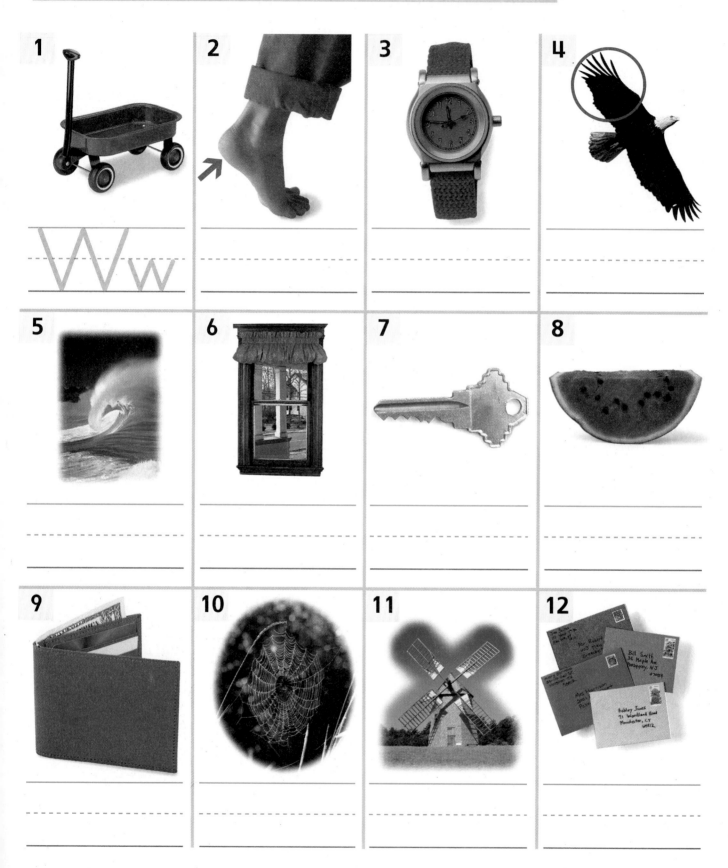

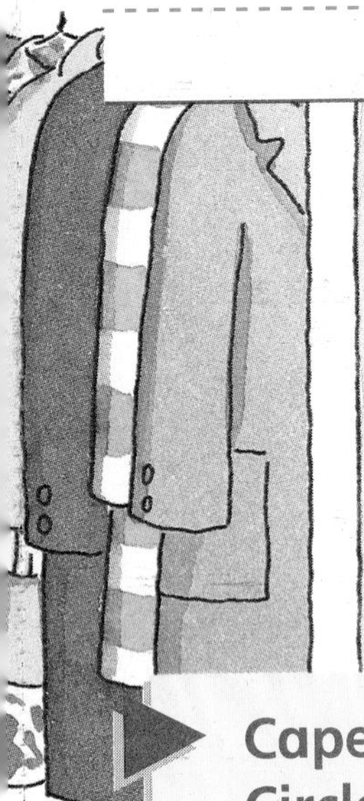

Carla has a cape.
She's carrying a cane.
Cory has her dad's coat
To play a dress-up game.

Cape **begins with the sound of c.**
**Circle each picture whose name
begins with the sound of c.**

1

2

3

4

5

6

7

8

9

Say the name of each picture. If it begins with the sound of **c**, print **Cc** on the line.

1	**2**	**3**	**4**
Cc			
5	**6**	**7**	**8**
9	**10**	**11**	**12**

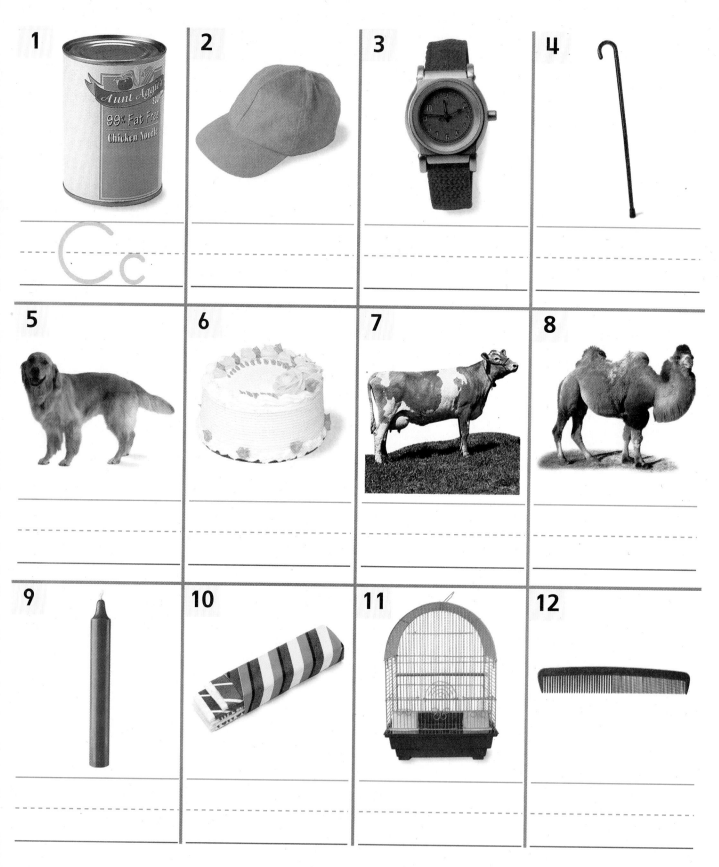

Lesson 23
The sound of c

Name a picture and ask your child to tell whether it begins with the same sound as *can*.

Row, row, row.
We row our red boat.
Row, row, row.
Our red boat can float.

▶ **Row** begins with the sound of **r**. **Circle** each picture whose name begins with the sound of **r**.

1
2
3
4
5
6
7
8
9

Lesson 24
The sound of r: Phonemic awareness

51

Say the name of each picture. If it begins with the sound of **r**, print **Rr** on the line.

1

_R r_

2

3

4

5

6

7

8

9

10

11

12

Lesson 24
The sound of r

 Home

Have your child say the name of each picture that begins with the sound of *r*.

Say the name of each picture. **Print** the letter for its beginning sound on the line. **Trace** the whole word.

1	2	3	4
eaf	at	ip	ing

5	6	7	8
og	ine	id	up

9	10	11	12
eb	at	oll	et

Say the name of each picture. **Draw** a line to match the puzzle pieces whose names begin with the same sound.

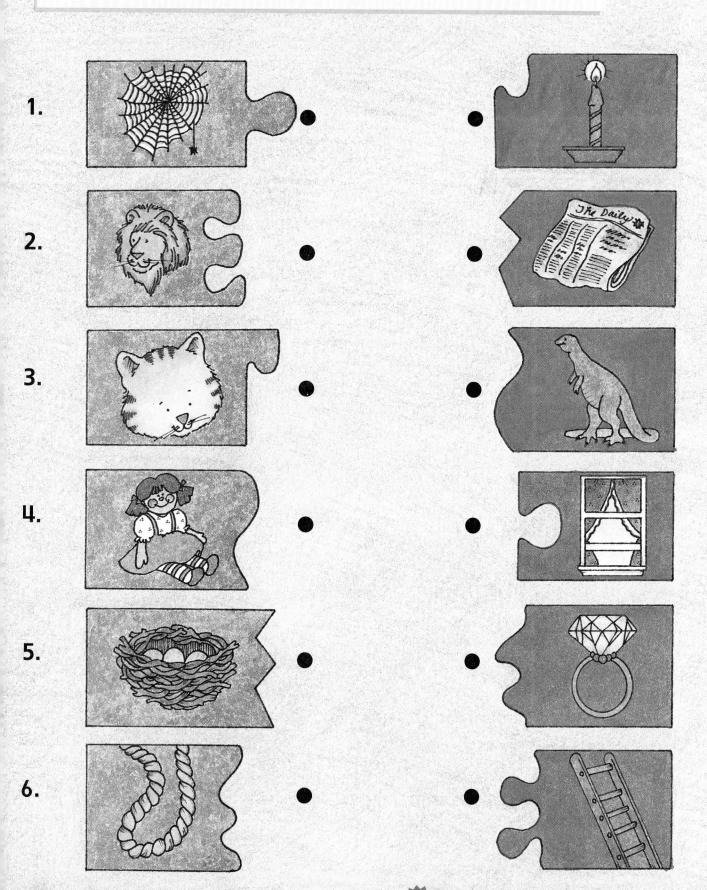

1.

2.

3.

4.

5.

6.

Lesson 25
Review consonants l, d, n, w, c, r

Home

Ask your child to tell you what letter each picture name begins with.

Penny passed the peach pie,
Peach pie, peach pie.
Penny passed the peach pie,
Till not a piece was left.

Pie **begins with the sound of p.** Circle **each picture whose name begins with the sound of p.**

1

2

3

4

5

6

7

8

9

Say the name of each picture. If it begins with the sound of **p**, print **Pp** on the line.

1	**2**	**3**	**4**
Pp			
5	**6**	**7**	**8**
9	**10**	**11**	**12**

Lesson 26
The sound of p

 Home

You and your child can take turns
saying the names of pictures whose
names begin with the sound of *p*.

Quinn's toy duck said,
"Quack, quack, quack!"
"Quiet!" said Quincy.
But the duck quacked back!

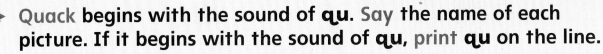

Quack **begins with the sound of** qu. **Say the name of each picture. If it begins with the sound of** qu, **print** qu **on the line.**

1

qu

2

3

4

5

6

7

8

Viv has a valentine.
Val has one, too.
Van makes a valentine
To give to you.

Valentine **begins with the sound of v.** Say
the name of each picture. If it begins with
the sound of **v**, print **Vv** on the line.

1	2	3	4
Vv			

5	6	7	8

9	10	11	12

Lesson 27
The sound of v: Phonemic awareness

Home

Point to the letters your child wrote
and ask her or him to name the
picture.

Say the name of each picture. Print the letter for its beginning sound on the first line. Then print the letter for its ending sound on the second line.

1

r | n

2

3

4

5

6

7

8

9

10

11

12

Review consonants w, c, r, p, q, v

1. h o

2. a

3. a n

4. e b

5. f i e

6. u e e n

7. n e

Lesson 28
Review consonants w, c, r, p, q, v

Ask your child what the secret
message is.

Zz go together.
Zz are partner letters.

▶ **Color each animal that has partner letters on it.**

**Draw a line from each yo-yo to its partner letter.
Color the yo-yo and the partner letter the same.**

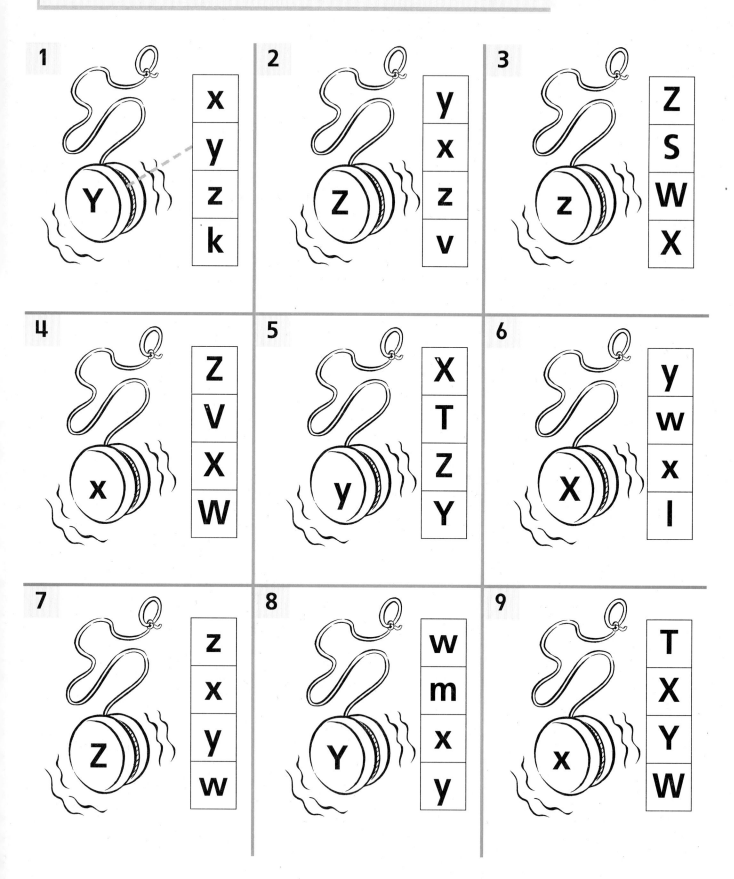

1.
Y

x
y
z
k

2.
Z

y
x
z
v

3.
Z

Z
S
W
X

4.
x

Z
V
X
W

5.
y

X
T
Z
Y

6.
X

y
w
x
l

7.
Z

z
x
y
w

8.
Y

w
m
x
y

9.
x

T
X
Y
W

Lesson 29
Partner letters Xx, Yy, Zz

Print a capital letter from the page
and ask your child to print the
matching small letter.

Will Foxie Fox and Oxie Ox
Fit inside our big toy box?
Mix things up and push and pull.
Fox and Ox make the toy box full!

▶ **Box** ends with the sound of **x.** Circle each picture whose name ends with the sound of **x.**

1

2

3

4

5

6

7

8

9

Yesterday I went shopping
With my Grandma Lin.
I got a yellow yo-yo.
You can watch it spin.

▶ **Yo-yo** begins with the sound of **y**. Say the name of each picture. Circle the beginning letter. Then circle each picture whose name begins with the sound of **y**.

1

Y
X
W
V

2

V
X
Y
W

3

B
Y
R
N

4

V
R
B
Y

5

R
F
Y
X

6

W
V
B
Y

Lesson 30
The sound of y: Phonemic awareness

Home

Name a picture. Have your child tell what letter stands for the beginning sound.

Zelda and Zena
Went to the zoo.
There they saw zebras
And lions, too.

▶ **Zoo** begins with the sound of **z.** Say the name of each picture. Fill in the bubble beside its beginning letter. Then circle each picture whose name begins with the sound of **z.**

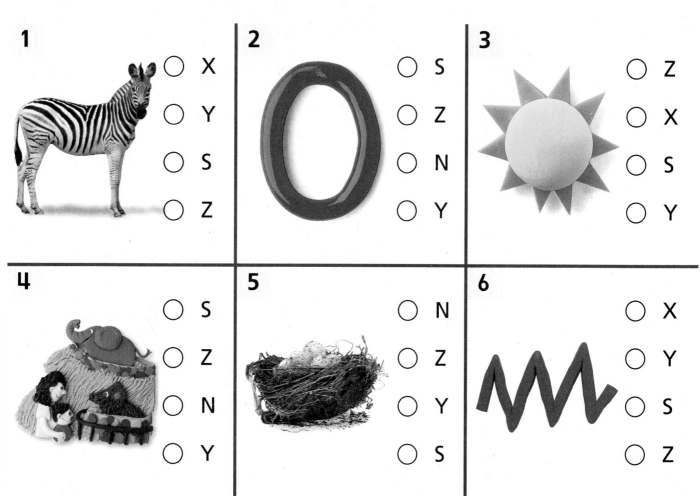

1
○ X
○ Y
○ S
○ Z

2
○ S
○ Z
○ N
○ Y

3
○ Z
○ X
○ S
○ Y

4
○ S
○ Z
○ N
○ Y

5
○ N
○ Z
○ Y
○ S

6
○ X
○ Y
○ S
○ Z

Say the name of each picture. If the name begins with the sound of the letter in the box, **print** it on the first line. If it ends with that sound, **print** it on the second line.

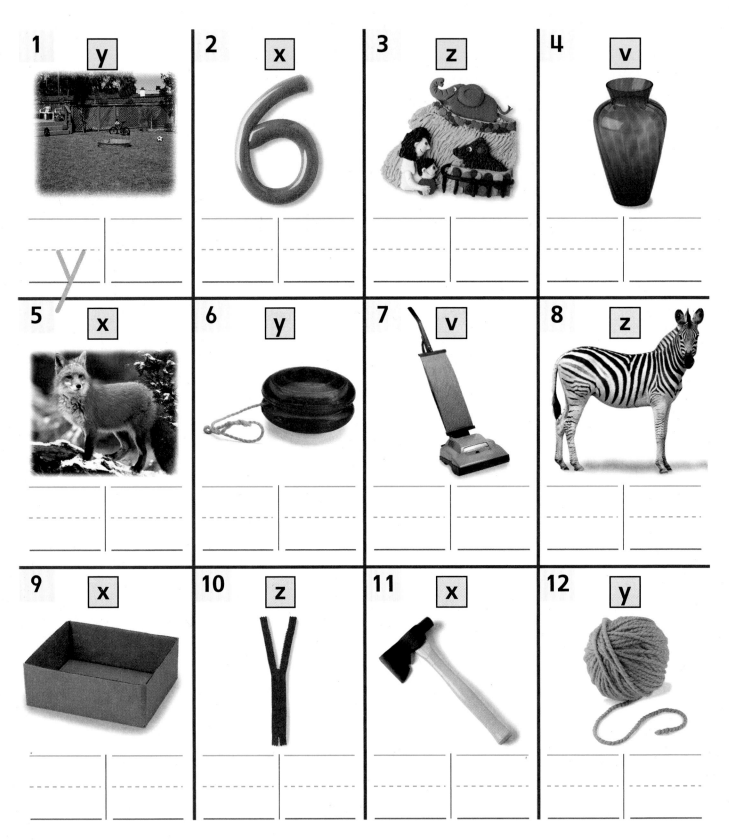

1 | y |

2 | x |

3 | z |

4 | v |

5 | x |

6 | y |

7 | v |

8 | z |

9 | x |

10 | z |

11 | x |

12 | y |

Lesson 31
Review consonants x, y, z

Say the name of each picture. **Print** the letter for its middle sound on the line.

1	2	3
4	5	6
7	8	9
10	11	12

Say the name of each picture. **Print** the letter for its middle sound on the line. **Trace** the whole word.

1

baby

2

po___y

3

ra___io

4

wa___on

5

ru___er

6

le___on

7

se___en

8

ro___ot

9

ti___er

Say a picture name and ask your child what letter stands for the middle sound.

 **Phonics & Spelling**

Say the name of each picture. Print the letter for its beginning sound. Then print the letter for its ending sound.

Word List	bed	cat	fox	ham	jar	king
	pig	queen	tub	van	web	yard

1

van

2

i

3

o

4

u

5

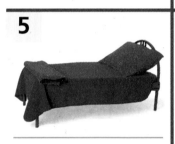

e

6

a

7

a

8

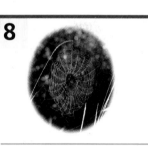

e

9

a

10

in

11

ar

12

uee

Phonics & Writing

▶ **Draw** a picture of your family.
Write a sentence about the picture.

Book Corner

Eight Friends in All
by Iris Littleman

Friends join each other. They have fun doing many things together.

Lesson 33
Review consonants: Writing

6

Dad looks in the yard, but no Socks.

SOCKS!

FOLD

8

What did Socks do on moving day?

TALK ABOUT IT

FOLD

3

Jon looks in a box, but no Socks.

1

This book belongs to:

FAMILY MOVING DAY

Lesson 34
Review consonants: Take-Home Book

 Say the name of each picture. **Print** the letter for the missing sound to finish each word.

1	**2**	**3**
arn	bu	ase
4	**5**	**6**
ha	ire	eart
7	**8**	**9**
ug	ebra	pe
10	**11**	**12**
ueen	agon	tu

Lesson 35
Consonants: Checkup

73

Say the name of each picture. Fill in the bubble next to the letter that stands for the beginning sound.

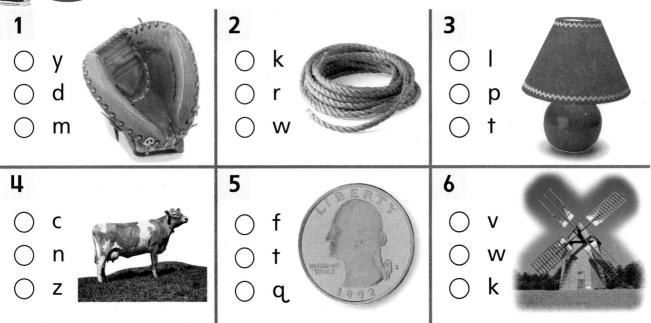

1
- ○ y
- ○ d
- ○ m

2
- ○ k
- ○ r
- ○ w

3
- ○ l
- ○ p
- ○ t

4
- ○ c
- ○ n
- ○ z

5
- ○ f
- ○ t
- ○ q

6
- ○ v
- ○ w
- ○ k

Say the name of each picture. Fill in the bubble next to the letter that stands for the ending sound.

7
- ○ k
- ○ z
- ○ x

8
- ○ g
- ○ c
- ○ z

9
- ○ n
- ○ p
- ○ r

10
- ○ f
- ○ n
- ○ q

11
- ○ d
- ○ t
- ○ j

12
- ○ k
- ○ l
- ○ w

UNIT 2

Short Vowels

Theme: Amazing Animals

Sing Along

The Itsy Bitsy Cricket

The itsy-bitsy cricket
Went hopping on a log.
The itsy-bitsy cricket
Met a hungry frog.
And while the frog was sitting
The cricket made a hop.
Ribbit!
The itsy-bitsy cricket
Decided not to stop.

 **Find the animals in the picture and say their names.**

THINK! **Why do you think the cricket did not stop?**

Home Letter

Dear Family,

The sounds that short vowels make are what we will be learning about in the next few weeks. Here are some examples.

a
cat

e
hen

i
pig

o
dog

u
duck

As you can see, many animal names contain short vowel sounds. In this unit we will be learning about all kinds of animals.

At-Home Activities

Here are some simple, fun activities you and your child can do at home to practice short vowel sounds.

▶ Ask your child to draw a picture of an animal that she or he considers amazing and to give the animal a special short vowel name.

▶ Make a collage of animals whose names have a short vowel sound. Cut pictures from old magazines or newspapers and glue them on paper, one sheet for each vowel. You can make the collage into a mobile by hanging the pages from a wire hanger with string or yarn.

Book Corner

You and your child might enjoy reading these books together. Look for them in your local library.

Crocodile Beat
by Gail Jorgensen

Crocodile is asleep, but the other animals are noisily heading down to the river. When Crocodile wakes up, he's ready for a meal!

The Animals
by Michio Mado

This collection of animal poems simply and humorously describes our furry and feathered friends.

Sincerely,

Look at the letter in each row. **Circle** each picture whose name has that letter.

1

a

cat   box   ax   cub

2

i

jug   igloo   mitt   lid

3

u

cup   duck   fan   umbrella

4

o

apple   puppy   top   ox

5

e

dress   egg   ant   bed

Look at the letter in the first box. Circle that letter each time you see it in the words.

1 **a**	c(a)p	at	lamp	hand
	and	plant	apple	papa

2 **i**	l(i)ps	gift	mitt	ring
	quilt	million	tiptop	ticket

3 **u**	(u)p	duck	nuts	scrub
	sunny	hugs	under	bump

4 **o**	(o)ff	mom	ox	stop
	pond	sock	frost	doctor

5 **e**	n(e)t	help	bell	rest
	egg	seven	camel	pencil

Home · Ask your child to write his or her name and identify the vowels in it.

An ant can dance.
An ant can sing.
An ant can do most anything.

Can you dance?
Can you sing?
Can you do most anything?

▶ **Ant** has the short sound of **a**. **Circle** each picture whose name has the short sound of **a**.

Say the names of the pictures in each row.
Color the pictures whose names rhyme.

1

  (row 1: pan, rat, axe, cat)

2

    (row 2: man, can, fan, lamp)

3

    (row 3: tag, tack, bag, ant)

4

    (row 4: ram, dad, ham, lamb)

5

    (row 5: bat, cap, map, hand)

Lesson 37
Short vowel a: Phonograms

 Home

Ask your child to name one or more
pictures whose names rhyme.

Say the name of each picture. Circle its name.

1	2	3
bat bad ban	ant wax ax	nap can cat

4	5	6
cab cap nap	man bag band	tag rag tap

7	8	9
fat fan tan	had hand land	tap lap lamp

10	11	12
van had ran	bad cab dad	pat pan ran

Read the words in the blue box. **Print** a word in the puzzle to name each picture.

Across →

2.

5.

6.

Down ↓

1.

3.

4.

1.

2.

3.

4.   5.

6.

bag	cat	hand
hat	map	pan

▶ **Use** some of the words from the box to write a sentence.

_____

- -

_____

_____

- -

_____

82 Lesson 38
Short vowel a

Home Make up riddles using some of the words from the box. Ask your child to guess the word.

Blend the letter sounds together as you say each word. Then **color** the picture it names.

1

v an

2

c ap

3

h am

4

b at

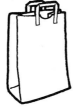  

5

c an

Blend the letter sounds together as you say each word. **Print** the word on the line. **Draw** a line to the picture whose name rhymes.

1

m ap

_____

map ●

2

r at

_____

●

3

h am

_____

●

4

t ag

_____

●

5

r an

_____

●

6

s ad

_____

●

Lesson 39
Short a: Blending/phonograms

Say a picture name and ask your child to name a word that rhymes.

Look at the picture. **Circle** the word that will finish the sentence. **Print** it on the line.

1. Max is my _____.
   - cat
   - sat
   - can

2. He licks my _____.
   - land
   - hand
   - ham

3. Max sits on my _____.
   - pad
   - rap
   - lap

4. He likes my _____.
   - sad
   - dad
   - bad

5. He plays with a _____.
   - bat
   - rag
   - bag

6. Max takes a _____.
   - nap
   - cap
   - cab

 **THINK!**

Why does the girl like Max?

Say the name of each picture. Print the letter for its beginning sound. Then print the letter for its ending sound.

1

cat

2

a

3

a

4

a

5

a

6

a

7

a

8

a

9

a

10

a

11

a

12

a

13

a

14

a

15

a

16

a

Lesson 40
Short a words: Spelling

Ask your child to read the story on page 85.

Read the sentences. Circle the word that will finish each sentence. Print it on the line.

1. Jan wanted to go to _____.

cap
camp
lamp

2. Dad and Jan got in the _____.

can
van
cat

3. Dad got gas and a _____.

tap
nap
map

4. At camp, Jan made a name _____.

tag
rag
tan

5. She made a mask from a _____.

wag
bat
bag

6. Jan even played in the _____.

band
can
wag

 **THINK!** Do you think Jan had fun at camp? Why?

Say the name of each picture. Print the picture name on the line. In the last box, draw a picture of a short **a** word. Write the word.

1

fan

2

3

4

5

6

7

8

9

10

11

12

Lesson 41
Short vowel a: Spelling

 Home
Point to a word and ask your child to say and spell a word that rhymes.

Read **the story. Use short a words to** finish the sentences.

LOOKING AT ANTS

Dan sat with his dad.
They saw some ants.
How fast they ran!

Ants ran in the sand.
Ants ran in the grass.
The ants were home at last!

1. Dan was with his _____.

2. They saw some _____.

3. Ants ran in the _____ and _____.

THINK! **Where do the ants run?**

Lesson 42
Review short vowel a: Reading

89

Look at the picture. **Write** about what you see. The words in the box may help you.

ants

ax

bag

camp

cap

dad

Lesson 42
Review short vowel a: Writing

Home Ask your child what he or she might like to do on a camping trip.

TALK ABOUT IT

Tell what you like about bats.

8

ALL About BATS

Written by Jennifer Jacobson
Photographs by Dr. Merlin Tuttle

This book belongs to:

1

Bats can have red fur.

6

Do you know that bats can fly fast and far?

3

What do you know
about bats?

2

Bats can have black or
brown fur.

7

Bats catch and eat a
lot of bugs.

4

Bats eat plants, too.

5

FOLD

Lesson 43
Review short vowel a: Take-Home Book

A big pink pig
Ate a big fig,
Put on a big wig,
And did a jig.

▶ **Pig** has the short sound of **i**. **Circle** each picture whose name has the short sound of **i**.

1

2

3

4

5

6

7

8

9

10

11

12

1

2

 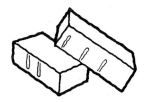  

3

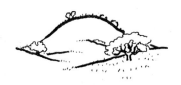   

4

 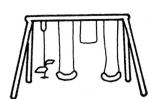  

5

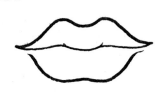   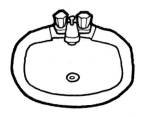

Lesson 44
Short vowel i: Phonograms

Point to a picture. Ask your
child to say a word that rhymes
with the picture name.

Say the name of each picture. Circle its name.

1

dig   big   pig

2

six   ax   mix

3

hid   lid   did

4

bib   bid   bad

5

fin   pin   pan

6

fill   hill   bill

7

mix   mat   mitt

8

sing   sank   sink

9

will   milk   mitt

10

win   fin   fan

11

fist   fish   fast

12

win   wing   ring

Farmer Jim's pigs have short **i** words on them. Help Farmer Jim catch his pigs. **Circle** the short **i** words.

pin

cat

six

big

tag

sink

lips

lid

pan

fan

bib

hill

Home

With your child, take turns making up riddles for each short *i* word and pointing to the answer.

Blend the letter sounds together as you say each word. Then **color** the picture it names.

1

w ig →

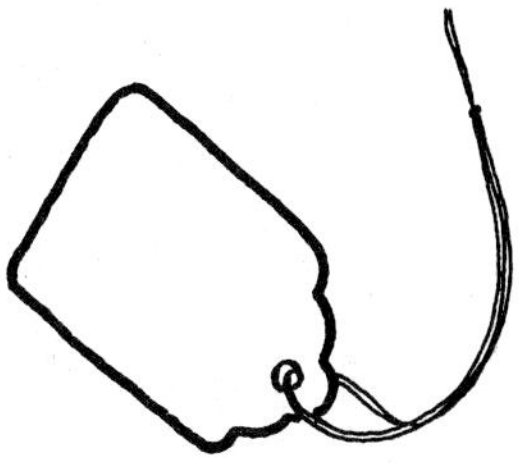

2

m ap →

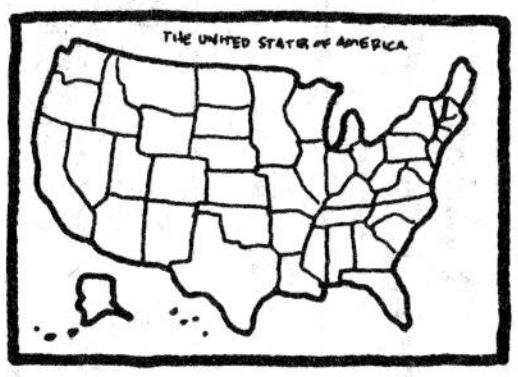

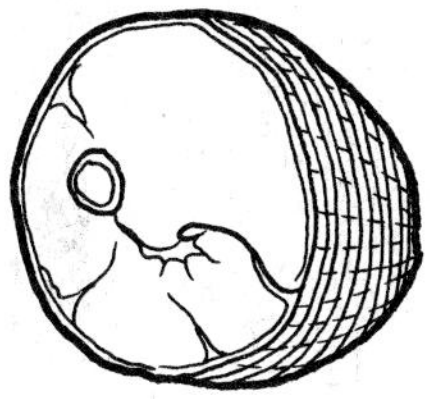

3

p in →

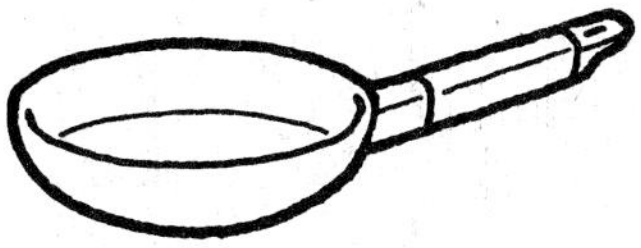

4

b ib →

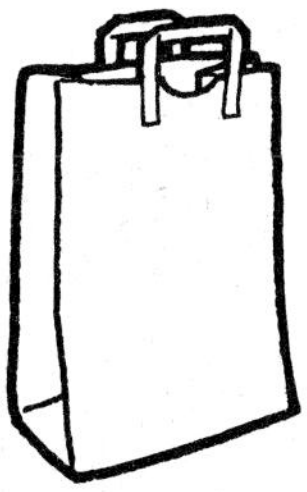

5

m an →

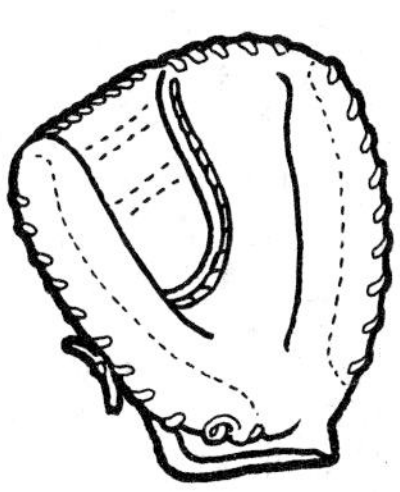

Print the word on the line.
Draw a line to the picture it names.

6

1

p ig _____

2

p an _____

3

s ix _____

4

c ap _____

5

r at _____

6

r ip _____

Lesson 46
Short vowels a, i: Blending/phonograms

Home

Ask your child to think of a
rhyming word for three of the
picture names.

Look at the picture. **Circle** the word that will finish the sentence. **Print** it on the line.

1. I got a _____.

_____

gap
gift
gum

2. Is it a _____?

_____

milk
mitt
tip

3. Does it drink _____?

_____

milk
mitt
mat

4. Will it fit on a _____?

_____

damp
dig
dish

5. Can it swim in the _____?

_____

sick
sink
sank

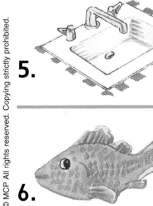

6. It is a _____!

_____

fist
fast
fish

THINK! Did you ever get a pet as a gift? Tell about it.

Lesson 47
Short vowel i: Words in context

99

1 wig

2 i

3 i

4 i

5 i

6 i

7 i

8 if

9 in

10 il

11 ip

12 in

13 i

14 i

15 in

16 is

Ask your child to use three of the words in sentences.

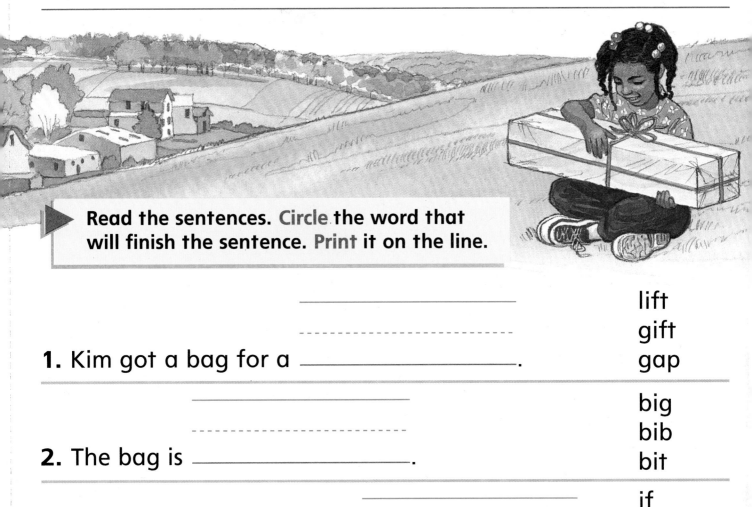

**Read the sentences. Circle the word that
will finish the sentence. Print it on the line.**

1. Kim got a bag for a _____.

                                              lift
gift
gap

2. The bag is _____.

                big
bib
bit

3. She has a bat and mitt in _____.

                if
is
it

4. The bag fell down the _____.

                bill
hit
hill

5. Now it has a little _____.

                tip
rip
him

6. She can fix it with a _____.

                pin
pan
fin

THINK! **What school things would
you put in a big bag?**

Lesson 48
Short vowel i: Words in context

101

Say the name of each picture. **Print** the picture name on the line. In the last box, draw a picture of a short **i** word. **Print** the picture name.

1
lid

2

3

4

5

6

7

8

9

10

11

12

Lesson 48
Short vowel i: Spelling

 Home

Discuss the picture your child drew in the last box and have him or her say the picture name.

 **Phonics & Reading**

▶ **Read** the story. **Print short i** words to finish the sentences.

SWIFT PIGS

Do you think pigs are slow?
This is not so!
A pig can be very quick.
Little pigs run in races.
Which pig will win?
The one that zips around the ring.

1. Some little _____ race on a track.

2. A quick pig can _____ a race.

3. The winning pig zips around the _____.

 **Why might people think pigs are slow?**

Lesson 49
Review short i: Reading
103

Phonics & **Writing**

Pretend you saw the pig race. Write about your day. The words in the box may help you.

| big |
| pig |
| win |
| ring |
| thing |
| quick |

Home

Ask your child to read aloud his or her story.

TALK ABOUT IT

Why did Jill think Bam did the bad things?

8

BiFF AND BAM

This book belongs to:

1

Biff tips over the big can.

6

Bam laps up the milk. "Bad Bam!" Jill says.

3

FOLD

FOLD

Biff bats at the milk.

2

Biff is bad, not Bam.
"Bad Biff!" Jill says.

7

Biff rips the mat.

4

Bam sits on the mat.
"Bad Bam!" Jill says.

5

Lesson 50
Review short vowels a, i: Take-Home Book

Rub-a-dub-dub.
The cub is in the tub.
Rub-a-dub-dub.
The cub likes to scrub.

▶ Cub has the short sound of **u**.
Circle each picture whose name
has the short sound of **u**.

1

2

3

4

5

6

7

8

9

10

11

12

Say the names of the pictures in each row.
Color the pictures whose names rhyme.

1
  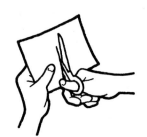 

2
  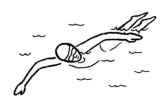 

3

4

5
 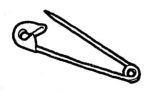  

Lesson 51
Short vowel u: Phonograms

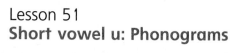 Ask your child to name the
rhyming pictures.

► **Say** the name of each picture. **Circle** its name.

1

suds   sand   (sun)

2
gum   mug   gust

3
cut   cap   cup

4
bun   bus   sun

5
bag   bug   big

6
but   tab   tub

7
jug   jack   gum

8
huts   mugs   nuts

9
tuck   duck   luck

10
mug   rug   rag

11
cub   cup   club

12
drum   dip   mad

Help the cub get home. Draw a line from the cub to the first word with the short **u** sound. Draw a line to each short **u** word. Then the cub will see its mom!

fox

fun

jug

jam

bug

bed

web

nut

dog

sun

cat

rug

mug

tub

Lesson 52
Short vowel u

Home

With your child, take turns naming
short *u* words.

Blend the letter sounds together as you say each word. **Color** the picture it names.

1   b ug

2   c an

3   p in

4   t ub

5   r at

6   w ig

Blend the letters to say each word. **Print** the word on the line. **Draw** a line to the picture it names.

1

b at →

●

2

s ix →

●

3

r ug →

●

4

p ig →

●

5

p an →

●

6

c ub →

●

Lesson 53
Short vowels a, i, u: Blending/phonograms

Home

Ask your child to say and spell each word.

Look at the picture. **Circle** the word that will finish the sentence. **Print** it on the line.

1. Gus sits on the _____ .

rub
rug
jug

2. He plays with his _____ .

pup
up
cup

3. Soon Gus sees the _____ .

bud
bug
bus

4. He jumps _____ .

hug
up
cup

5. Gus has to _____ .

rub
fun
run

6. The bus is stuck in the _____ !

mud
mug
hum

What do you think will happen next?

Lesson 54
Short vowel u: Words in context

113

Say the name of each picture. **Print** the letter for its beginning sound. Then **print** the letter for its ending sound. In the last box, **draw** a picture of a short **u** word. **Print** the picture name.

1 cup	2 u	3 u	4 u
5 u	6 u	7 u	8 u
9 u	10 u	11 u	12 u
13 u	14 u	15 u	16

Lesson 54
Short vowel u: Spelling

 Home

Ask your child to use three of the words in sentences.

Circle the word that will finish the sentence. **Print** it on the line.

1. Our farm is _____.

fan
fin
fun

2. I looked under trees for _____.

nuts
buns
suns

3. Bugs buzz and _____.

hut
hand
hum

4. The pigs dig in the _____.

must
mud
mug

5. My dog jumps and _____.

runs
rings
hugs

6. He likes the warm _____.

gum
sun
hum

THINK! What are some things you might do at a farm?

Lesson 55
Short vowel u: Words in context

115

Say the name of each picture. **Print** the picture name on the line. In the last box, **draw** a picture of a short **u** word. **Print** the picture name.

1

tub

2

3

4

5

6

7

8

9

10

11

12

Lesson 55
Short vowel u: Spelling

 Home

Point to a picture. Ask your child to name it and to spell the picture name.

Phonics & Reading

Read **the story.** Print **short u words** to finish the sentences.

The Cub and the Bug

"Life is dull," said the cub.
I must have some fun.
I'll have fun with this bug!"

"Buzz, buzz!" said the bug.
It stung the cub.
The sting made a big lump.

"Ow!" the cub said.
"That bug was not fun!"

1. The cub wanted to have _____.

2. The _____ stung the cub.

3. The cub had a big _____.

THINK! Why do you think the bug stung the cub?

Phonics & Writing

What could the cub do to have fun? **Write** the cub a letter. Tell him what you think. The words in the box may help you.

Dear Cub,

Your friend,

up
run
jump
hug
truck
mud

Lesson 56
Review short u: Writing

Home Ask your child to read the letter he or she wrote and explain his or her answer.

TALK ABOUT IT

What things do birds need to live?

8

LUNCH IN A JUG

This book belongs to:

1

Hang the jug from a branch.

6

FOLD

Scrub a milk jug. Clean it up.

3

You can be a bird pal.

Make a milk jug feeder.

2

FOLD

Fill the jug with nuts and seeds. Watch the fun!

7

Cut a hole in the jug.

4

FOLD

Tie thin string to the jug.

5

My dog has lots of spots.
My dog's spots look like dots.
My dog's spots are on his hair.
My dog's spots are everywhere!

▶ **Dog** has the short sound of **o**. **Circle** each
picture whose name has the short sound of **o**.

1

2

3

4

5

6

7

8

9

10

11

12

Say the names of the pictures in each row.
Color the pictures whose names rhyme.

1

2

3

4

 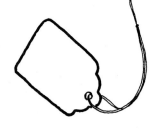  

5

Lesson 58
Short vowel o: Phonograms

 Home

Point to a picture. Ask your child to
name a word that rhymes.

Say the name of each picture. **Circle** its name.

1. top pot pack

2. box fox fog

3. log dog lot

4. nap map mop

5. tap tip top

6. hat hot hit

7. dog dig dug

8. bat box bug

9. fill duck doll

10. ox sock ax

11. rip rack rock

12. pop pup pat

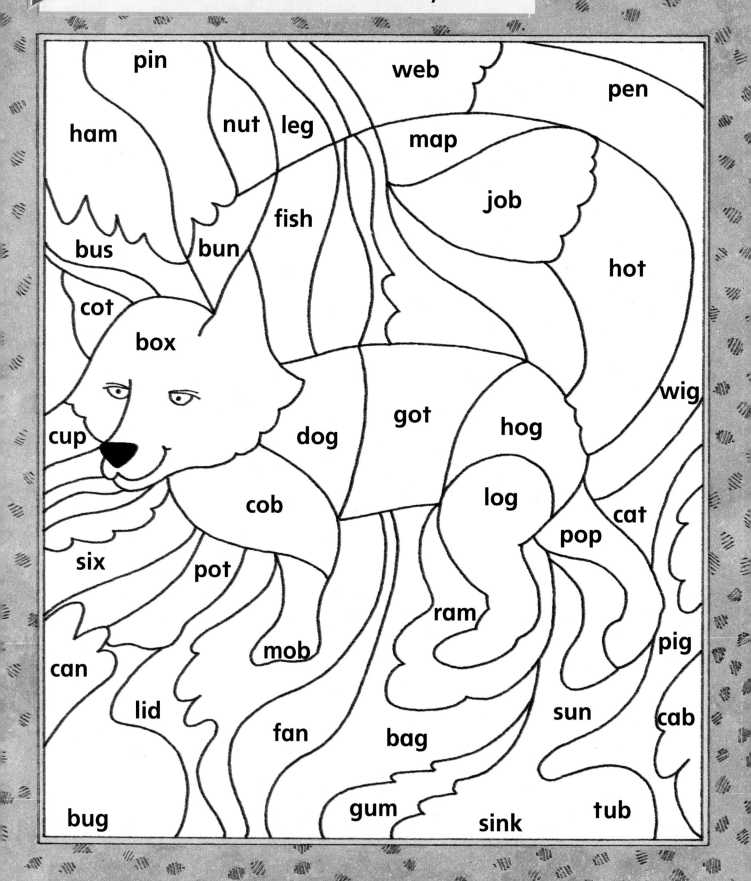

Lesson 59
Short vowel o

Home Ask your child what the picture shows and to spell the picture name.

Blend the letter sounds together as you say each word. **Color** the picture it names.

1 l og →

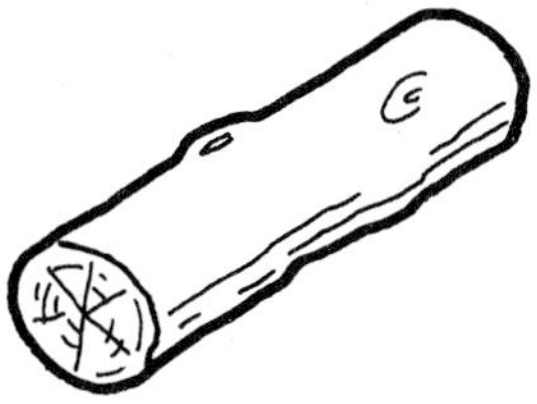

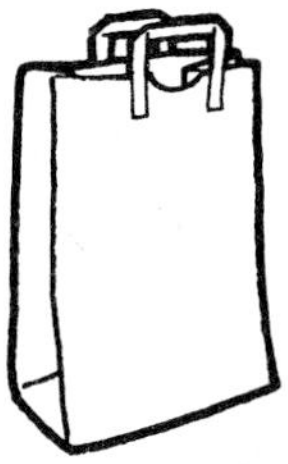

2 b at →

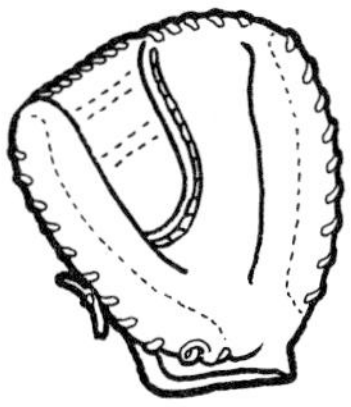

3 c ub →

4 f ox →

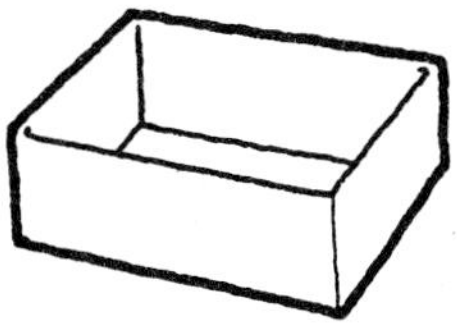

5 p in →

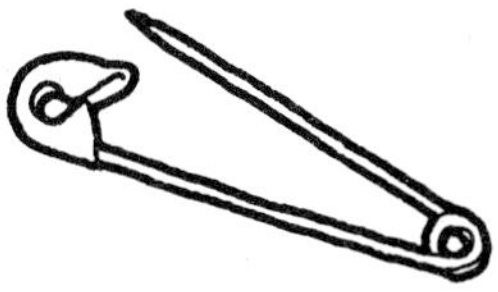

6 r ug →

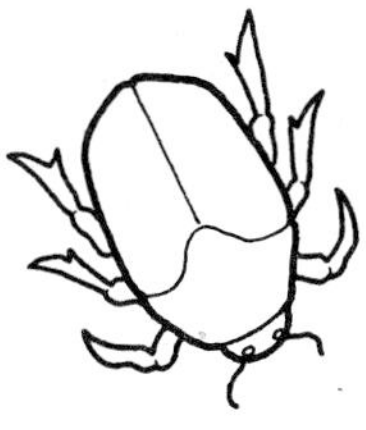

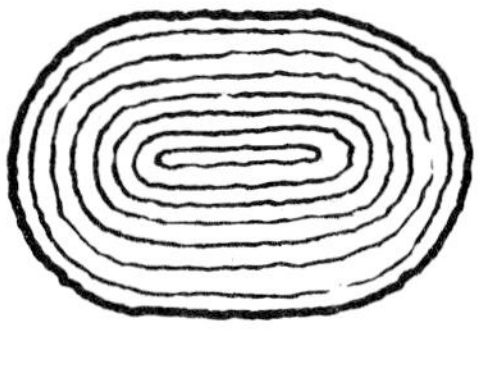

Blend the letter sounds together as you say each word. **Print** the word on the line. **Draw** a line to the picture it names.

1

b   ox   _____

2

s   ix   _____

3

c   up   _____

4

m   an   _____

5

d   og   _____

6

b   us   _____

Lesson 60
Short vowels a, i, u, o: Blending/phonograms

Home

Name the beginning letter of a word. Ask your child to read a word that starts with that letter.

Look at the picture. **Circle** the word that will finish the sentence. **Print** it on the line.

1. _____
   Bob is _____.

   hot
   got
   hop

2. _____
   He sits on top of a _____.

   rock
   rack
   lock

3. _____
   He takes off his _____.

   sacks
   socks
   locks

4. _____
   The grass is _____.

   sack
   lift
   soft

5. _____
   He sees a frog in the _____.

   pond
   pot
   pod

6. _____
   The frog hops on a _____.

   lock
   lost
   log

What do you think Bob might do next?

1 mop

2 o

3 oc

4 o

5 oc

6 o

7 ol

8 o

9 o

10 oc

11 o

12 o

13 o

14 o

15 ro

16 o

Discuss the picture your child drew in the last box. Ask him or her to say the picture name.

> **Circle** the word that will finish the sentence. **Print** it on the line.

1. Jill likes to _____.

job
jog
jug

2. She puts on shoes and _____.

sand
soft
socks

3. She jogs with her _____.

dot
dock
dog

4. She runs up to the hill _____.

top
tap
mop

5. It gets very _____.

hog
hit
hot

6. She _____ to rest.

sips
stops
steps

 **THINK!** What sports do you like?

Say the name of each picture. **Print** the picture name on the line. In the last box, **draw** a picture of a short **o** word. **Print** the picture name.

1	**2**	**3**
4	**5**	**6**
7	**8**	**9**
10	**11**	**12**

Lesson 62
Short vowel o: Spelling

 Home

Name a picture. Ask your child to name a picture that rhymes and write the rhyming word.

▶ **Read** the story. **Print short o** words to finish the sentences.

Foxes

Foxes live in many places.
Some live where it is hot.
Others live where it is cold.

Foxes are a lot like dogs.
Fox babies are called pups.
Foxes have soft fur.

_____

1. _____ live in many places.

2. Some live where it is _____.

3. Foxes are a lot like _____.

Look at the picture. **Write** about what you see. **The words in the box may help you.**

hop
fox
pond
frog
rock
top

Lesson 63
Review short o: Writing

Home

Ask your child to point to and say the short o words she or he has written.

Yum. Yum.

TALK ABOUT IT

How do some pond animals find food?

8

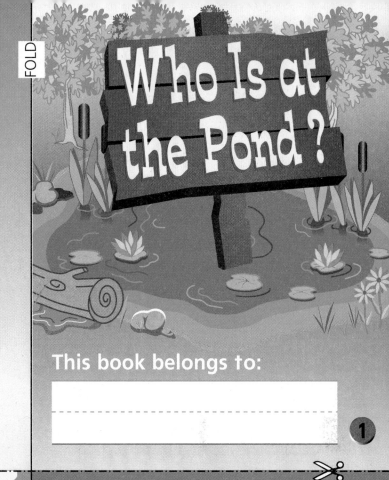

Who Is at the Pond?

This book belongs to:

1

A bug zips by.

Buzz. Buzz.

6

Quack. Quack.

A big duck and three little ducks swim by.

3

Review short vowels a, i, u, o: Take-Home Book

A frog sits on a lily pad in the warm sun.

The frog zaps the bug.

Two robins stop to drink and sing.

A turtle plops into the water.

"Red Hen, Red Hen,"
Jen said to her hen.
"Red Hen, Red Hen,
Get back to your pen!"

> **Hen** has the short sound of **e**. **Circle** each picture whose name has the short sound of **e**.

1	**2**	**3**	**4**
5	**6**	**7**	**8**
9	**10**	**11**	**12**

Say the names of the pictures in each row.
Color the pictures whose names rhyme.

1

  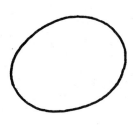 

2

   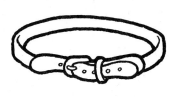

3

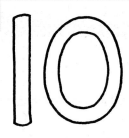   

4

5

Lesson 65
Short vowel e: Phonemic awareness

 Name a picture. Ask your child to
think of words that rhyme.

Say the name of each picture. Circle its name.

1
bed   fed   led

2
bill   sell   bell

3
tan   ten   tin

4
met   net   nut

5
west   well   web

6
jet   pet   wet

7
went   man   men

8
leg   egg   beg

9
ten   tent   bent

10
belt   bell   melt

11
pin   pet   pen

12
nest   not   just

Six silly red hens are missing from their pen. Draw a hen in each box. **Follow the directions below.**

1

Draw a red hen in a bed.

2

Draw a red hen in a tent.

3

Draw a red hen on a sled.

4

Draw a red hen dressed in a vest.

5

Draw a red hen getting all wet.

6

Draw a red hen with ten eggs.

**Blend the sounds together as you say each word.
Fill in the bubble under the picture it names.**

1 r ug ➡
   ○   ○   ○

2 t en ➡
   ○   ○   ○

3 s ix ➡
   ○   ○   ○

4 h at ➡
   ○   ○   ○

5 t op ➡
   ○   ○   ○

6 l eg ➡
   ○   ○   ○

Short vowels a, i, o, u, e: Blending/phonograms

Blend the sounds together as you say each word. **Print** the word on the line. **Draw** a line to the picture it names.

1

n   et

_____
- - - - - - - - - - - ●

2

m   op

_____
- - - - - - - - - - - ●

3

s   un

_____
- - - - - - - - - - - ●

4

w   ig

_____
- - - - - - - - - - - ●

5

c   at

_____
- - - - - - - - - - - ●

6

p   en

_____
- - - - - - - - - - - ●

 Name a vowel. Ask your child to read a word that has that vowel.

Look at the picture. **Circle** the word that will finish the sentence. **Print** it on the line.

1. Meg sits at her _____.
mask
desk
duck

2. She picks up her _____.
pen
pet
pig

3. Meg draws a _____.
best
nest
net

4. Then she draws a big _____.
leg
egg
beg

5. On the nest sits a _____.
hen
ten
pen

6. Meg hangs it by her _____.
belt
bell
bed

What kinds of things do you like to draw?

Lesson 68
Short vowel e: Words in context

141

Say the name of each picture. **Print** the letter for its beginning and ending sounds. In the last box, **draw** a picture of a short **e** word.

1	2	3	4
net	__ e __	__ e __	__ e __

5	6	7	8
__ e __	__ e __	__ e __	__ e __

9	10	11	12
e n __	__ e __	__ e s	e l

13	14	15	16
__ e s	__ e __	__ e s	__ e __

Lesson 68
Short vowel e: Spelling

Home

Say a picture name. Ask your child to name the beginning or ending letter.

142

Circle the word that will finish the sentence. **Print** it on the line.

1. Ted did not have a _____.

    sell
    sled
    sent

2. Ben _____ Ted use his sled.

    let
    leg
    lost

3. It _____ down the hill fast.

    went
    wet
    west

4. Peg let Ted use her sled _____.

    exit
    nest
    next

5. Her sled is as fast as a _____!

    just
    jet
    get

6. Ted likes Peg's sled the _____.

    bell
    best
    bent

THINK! Which sled would you like to use? Why?

Lesson 69
Short vowel e: Words in context
143

Say the name of each picture. Print the picture name on the line. In the last box, draw a picture of a short e word. Print the picture name.

1

_____
- - - - - - - - - - -
_____

2

_____
- - - - - - - - - - -
_____

3

_____
- - - - - - - - - - -
_____

4

_____
- - - - - - - - - - -
_____

5

_____
- - - - - - - - - - -
_____

6

_____
- - - - - - - - - - -
_____

7

_____
- - - - - - - - - - -
_____

8

_____
- - - - - - - - - - -
_____

9

_____
- - - - - - - - - - -
_____

10

_____
- - - - - - - - - - -
_____

11

_____
- - - - - - - - - - -
_____

12

_____
- - - - - - - - - - -
_____

 Lesson 69
Short vowel e: Spelling

144

 Say a picture name. Ask your child to point to the word and spell it.

Say the name of each picture. Circle the vowel you hear in its name. Print the word.

Word List

bag
bus
lid
map
pig
jet
cup
sock

1

a e i o u

_____

2

a e i o u

_____

3

a e i o u

_____

4

a e i o u

_____

5

a e i o u

_____

6

a e i o u

_____

7

a e i o u

_____

8

a e i o u

_____

 Phonics & Writing

 Write a postcard to tell a friend about a trip. Use some spelling words in your postcard.

cat	fan	bed	top	bug
dog	six	jet	pig	sun

USA 32

TO:

My Friend
1 Happy Lane
Yourtown,
USA
12345

Book Corner

When the Alligator Came to Class
by Cass Hollander

An alligator in the class
causes more trouble than you
could imagine.

 Home

Ask your child to spell the words
he or she wrote on page 145.

TALK ABOUT IT

Which fish do you think is the most amazing?

8

AMAZING FISH

This book belongs to:

1

Is this a frog?
No, it is a fish.

This fish can go fast on land!

6

FOLD

This fish can fish for a smaller fish.

3

This fish catches bugs. How?

Think about fish.
Fish are amazing!

2

It spits at them!

7

Fish can hide well!
Can you find a fish here?

Can you tell what
this fish is called?

4

5

Lesson 71
Review short vowels a, i, u, o, e: Take-Home Book

Say the name of each picture.
Print the picture name on the line.

1	2	3
bed		

4	5	6

7	8	9

10	11	12

UNIT 2 CHECKUP

Fill in the bubble beside the sentence that tells about the picture.

1

○ Pat has a fan.
○ Pam has fun.

2

○ Jan's pen is in a box.
○ Kim's pin is in a bag.

3

○ The gift is in the bag.
○ The quilt is on the bed.

4

○ The man set up the tent.
○ The men on the bus left.

5

○ Ned rang a bell on the desk.
○ Nick sat and fed a duck in the pond.

6

○ Miss Beck runs with the dog.
○ Jeff hugs his cat on the bed.

Lesson 72
Short vowels: Checkup

UNIT 3

Long Vowels

Theme: Let's Play

▶ **Find the hidden pictures of things you can play with.**

THINK! **What do you think the children will do to have fun?**

Home Letter

Dear Family,

Your child has begun to learn to read and write words with long vowel sounds such as the following.

a	e	i	o	u
skate	feet	bike	boat	flute

As you can see, many words related to leisure-time activities contain long vowel sounds. In this unit we will be focusing on different children's games, sports, and hobbies.

At-Home Activities

Here are some activities that you and your child might like to do together.

▶ With your child, look through old magazines and catalogs to find and cut out pictures of toys, games, sports equipment, and other things whose names have long vowel sounds. Ask your child to group the pictures according to the vowel sounds. For example, pictures of skates and a model train would go together, because skates and train have the long a sound.

▶ Ask your child to draw a picture of himself or herself playing a favorite sport or game. Help your child write a caption for the picture.

Book Corner

You and your child might enjoy reading these books together. Look for them in your local library.

Max
by Rachel Isadora

Max attends his sister's dancing class in order to warm up for his Saturday baseball game.

Max Found Two Sticks
by Brian Pinkney

Max finds two sticks and has fun communicating through music instead of words.

Sincerely,

Kay is down at the lake
With a pail and a rake.
She'll throw sticks for Jake
And laugh when he shakes.

▶ Lake **has the long sound of a.** Circle **each picture whose name has the long sound of a.**

1

2

3

4

5

6

7

8

9

10

11

12

Say the names of the pictures in each row.
Color the pictures whose names rhyme.

1

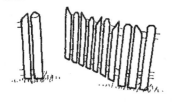 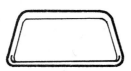 

2

3

4

5

Lesson 73
Long vowel a: Phonograms

 Home

Ask your child to suggest rhyming words for some of the picture names.

Say the name of each picture. **Circle** its name.

1

tape   tail   late

2

late   lake   rake

3

nail   rail   name

4

case   cap   cape

5

gave   game   name

6

made   mail   sail

7

gate   game   date

8

pain   ran   rain

9

van   save   vase

10

may   hay   way

11

Pail   Rain   Gail

12

play   pay   hay

Help **Kate** get to the game. **Read each** word.
Draw a line to join the long **a** words.

pig

cup

bat

vase

rake

mail

rain

tray

gate

cake

lid

pot

play

cap

rake

Lesson 74
Long vowel a

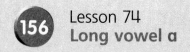

Ask your child to read the words along the path that leads to the soccer game.

Say the name of each picture. If the vowel sound is short, color the box with the word short. If the vowel sound is long, color the box with the word long.

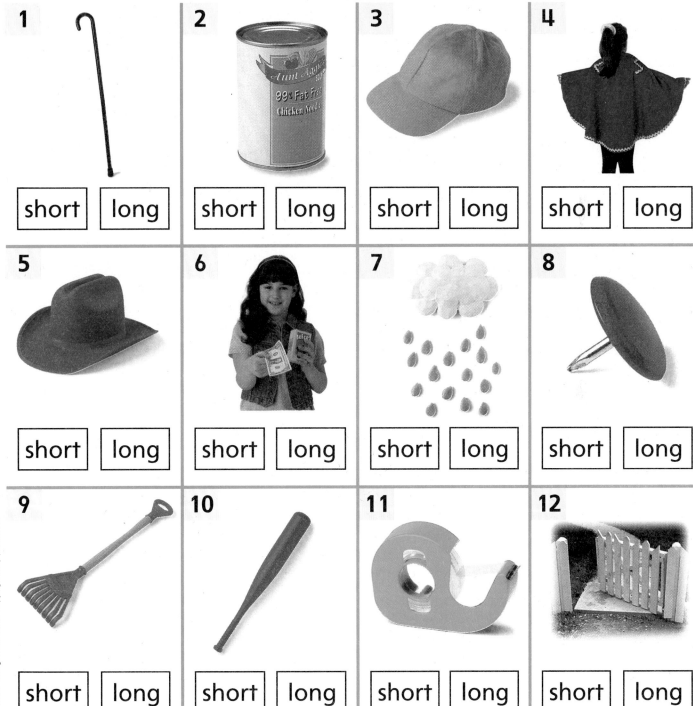

1	2	3	4
short long	short long	short long	short long

5	6	7	8
short long	short long	short long	short long

9	10	11	12
short long	short long	short long	short long

Help **Dave, Gail, and Ray** find the long **a** words.
Circle **each one you find.**

1

at	ate	rake	rack	page
made	safe	tap	tape	mad

Dave

2

rain	ram	wait	cat	pail
sat	sail	main	man	pal

Gail

3

May	man	pay	pat	play
day	damp	say	way	sand

Ray

Lesson 75
Long vowel a

 Home

Say a word or a picture name. Ask
your child whether the vowel sound
is long or short.

Say the name of each picture. **Circle** its name.

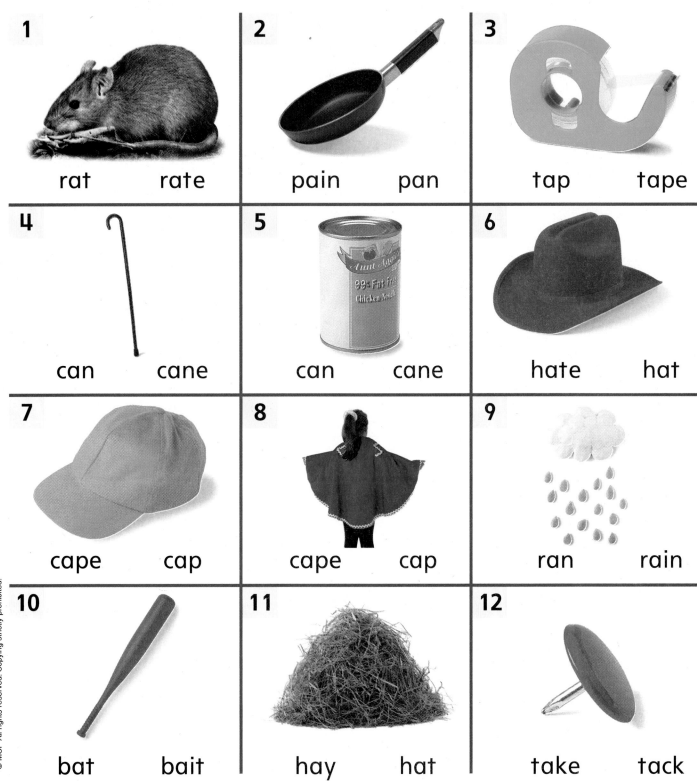

1 rat rate	**2** pain pan	**3** tap tape
4 can cane	**5** can cane	**6** hate hat
7 cape cap	**8** cape cap	**9** ran rain
10 bat bait	**11** hay hat	**12** take tack

Look at the picture. **Circle** the word that will finish the sentence. **Print** it on the line.

1. _____

_____ and Ray go out to play.

Save
Dave
Sand

2. _____

They go to the _____ .

lake
make
late

3. _____

They play a _____ .

gate
name
game

4. _____

Ray sits by a _____ .

save
came
cave

5. _____

Dave sees a boat with a _____ .

save
sail
mail

6. _____

They go in when it _____ .

rains
cane
ran

THINK! What are some things you might do at a lake?

Lesson 76
Long vowel a: Words in context

 Home

Ask your child to use the words circled on page 159 in sentences.

Say the name of each picture. Print the missing vowels on the line. In the last box, draw a picture whose name has the sound of long **a.** Print the name.

1

c a p e

2

c _ _ n

3

r _ _ n

4

v _ s _

5

g _ t _

6

_ _ k

7

b _ g

8

n _ _ l

9

c _ k _

10

m _ _ l

11

g _ m _

12

Lesson 77
Long vowel a: Spelling

161

Circle the word that will finish the sentence. Print it on the line.

1. The bus was _____.

lane
late
lake

2. Mom had to _____.

wait
wade
wake

3. Then she ran home in the _____.

rate
rake
rain

4. Mom came in by the _____.

gain
gate
game

5. She _____ me a big hug.

gave
gain
gate

6. I gave her the _____.

made
mail
make

 **How do you think Mom feels?**

Lesson 77
Long vowel a: Words in context

Home

Ask your child to read the three words in each box and to identify the long vowel sound.

Color each balloon that has three rhyming long **a** words.

1. game tame name

2. take tape ape

3. cane lane mane

4. sail same rail

5. cake rake lake

6. gate date late

7. fade made make

8. cave wave cake

9. bake fake fame

10. nail mail pail

11. rain gain pain

12. hay day pay

Say the name of each picture. **Print** the picture name on the line. In the last box, **draw** a picture of a long **a** word. **Print** the picture name.

1

_____

- - - - - - - - - - - -

_____

2

_____

- - - - - - - - - - - -

_____

3

_____

- - - - - - - - - - - -

_____

4

_____

- - - - - - - - - - - -

_____

5

_____

- - - - - - - - - - - -

_____

6

_____

- - - - - - - - - - - -

_____

7

_____

- - - - - - - - - - - -

_____

8

_____

- - - - - - - - - - - -

_____

9

_____

- - - - - - - - - - - -

_____

10

_____

- - - - - - - - - - - -

_____

11

_____

- - - - - - - - - - - -

_____

12

_____

- - - - - - - - - - - -

_____

Lesson 78
Long vowel a: Spelling

 Home
Point to a picture. Ask your child to read its name and then say a word that rhymes with it.

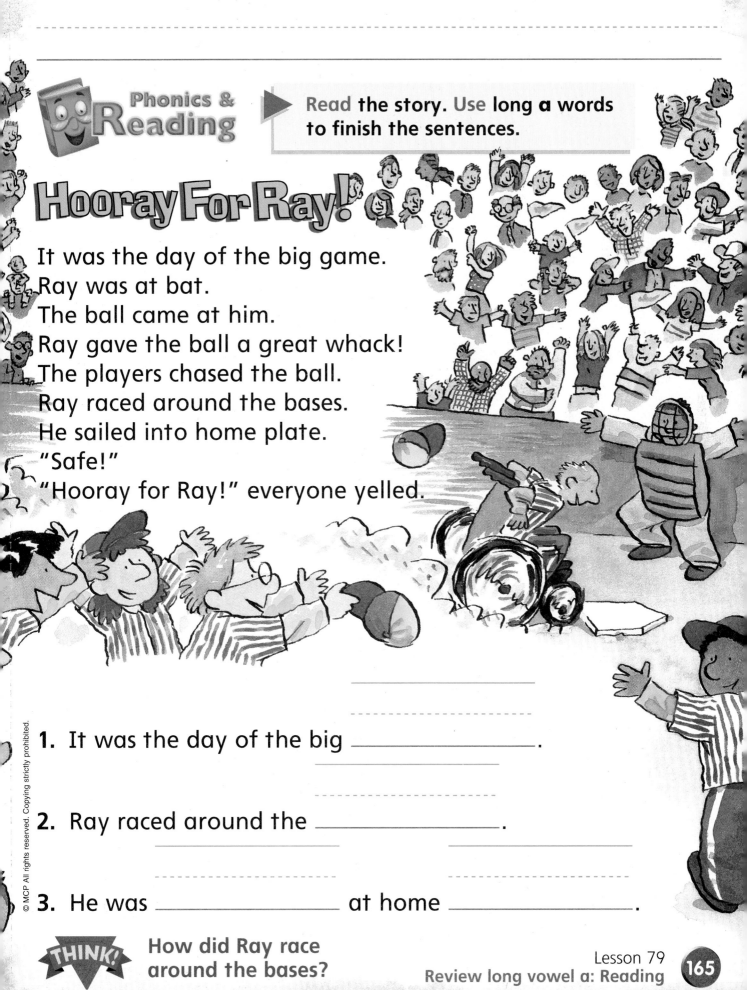

Phonics & Reading

Read **the story. Use long a words to finish the sentences.**

Hooray For Ray!

It was the day of the big game.
Ray was at bat.
The ball came at him.
Ray gave the ball a great whack!
The players chased the ball.
Ray raced around the bases.
He sailed into home plate.
"Safe!"
"Hooray for Ray!" everyone yelled.

1. It was the day of the big _____.

2. Ray raced around the _____.

3. He was _____ at home _____.

THINK! How did Ray race
around the bases?

Phonics & Writing

Write a story about the big game for a newspaper. **Make up** a good name for your story. **Use** some of your spelling words.

day	safe
race	wait	way

Lesson 79
Review long vowel a: Writing

 Home

Ask your child to read aloud the story on page 165.

6

Do not skate alone.
Skate with a pal.

8

Why should you
skate with a pal?

TALK
ABOUT IT

FOLD

FOLD

3

Thick pads
will help
make you
safe.

This book belongs to:

Safe
Skating

1

Lesson 80
Review long vowel a: Take-Home Book

Ride a bike.
Fly a kite.
Take a hike.
Say goodnight!

▶ **Ride** has the long sound of **i**. **Circle** each picture whose name has the long sound of **i**.

1	2	3	4
5	6	7	8
9	10	11	12

Say the names of the pictures in each row.
Color the pictures whose names rhyme.

1

2

3

4

5

6

Lesson 81
Long vowel i: Phonograms

Home

Ask your child to name all
the pictures that have a long *i*
vowel sound.

Say **the name of each picture.** Circle **its name.**

1

mine   nine   vine

2

dive   dine   dime

3

pin   pie   pine

4

ride   hide   ripe

5

bite   bike   kite

6

fine   fire   five

7

tie   ride   tire

8

bite   tide   bike

9

like   kite   tile

10

vine   wine   line

11

dive   dime   five

12

hide   ride   hit

Read the words in the box. **Print** a word in the puzzle to name each picture.

tie   bike   ride   ice
kite   mice   pie   dime

Across ▶

1.

3.

4.

7.

8.

Down ⬇

2.

5.

6.

Use some of the words from the box to write a sentence.

Lesson 82
Long vowel i

Ask your child to read aloud the sentence she or he wrote.

Say the name of each picture. If the vowel sound is short, **color** the box with the word short. If the vowel sound is long, **color** the box with long.

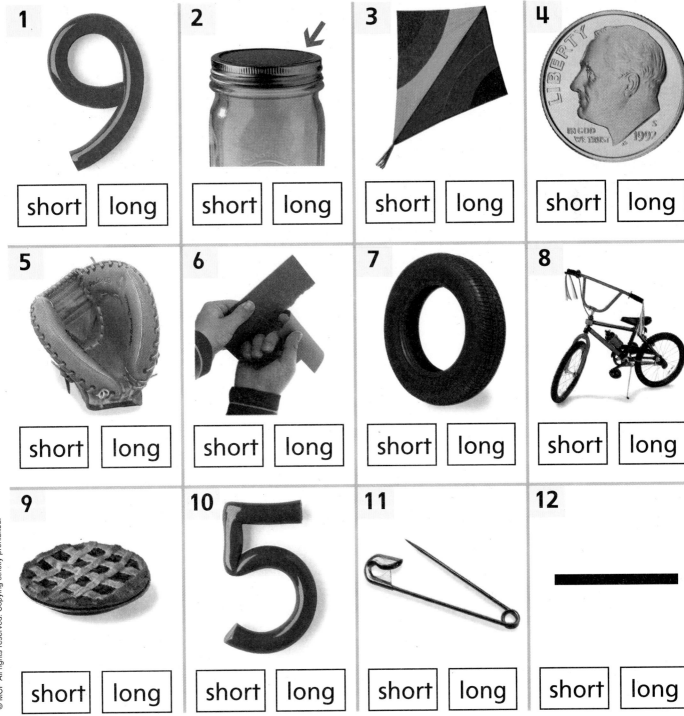

1	short | long
2	short | long
3	short | long
4	short | long
5	short | long
6	short | long
7	short | long
8	short | long
9	short | long
10	short | long
11	short | long
12	short | long

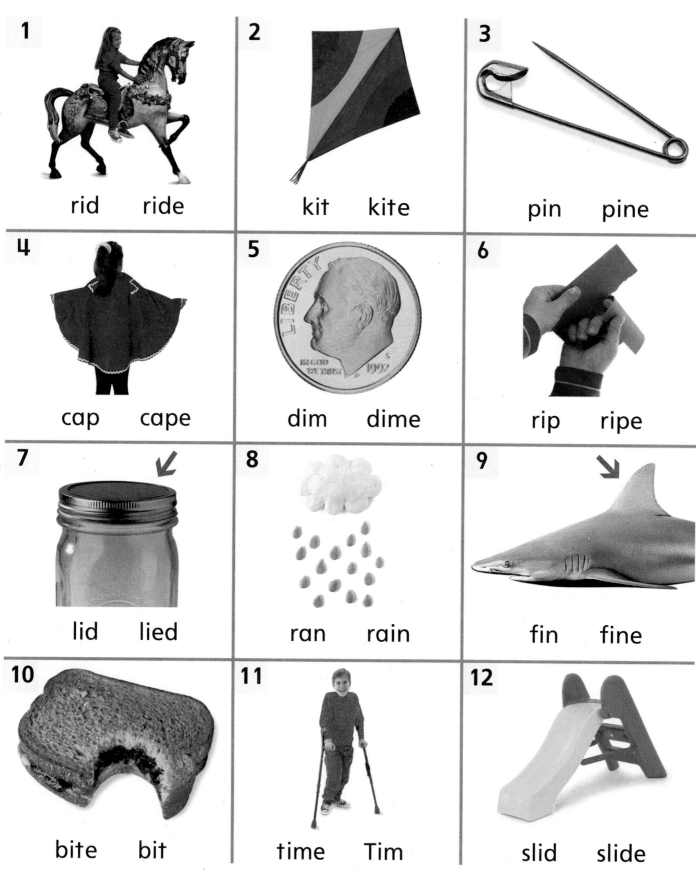

1 rid   ride

2 kit   kite

3 pin   pine

4 cap   cape

5 dim   dime

6 rip   ripe

7 lid   lied

8 ran   rain

9 fin   fine

10 bite   bit

11 time   Tim

12 slid   slide

 174

Lesson 83
Long vowel i: Picture-text match

 Home   Ask your child to read the two words under each picture and tell whether the vowel sound is short or long.

Look at the picture. Circle the word that will finish the sentence. Print it on the line.

1.  Jim has _____ dimes.

fine
file
five

2.  He will not get a _____.

kite
bite
bake

3.  Will he get a _____?

lie
pie
pile

4.  He waits in _____.

like
lied
line

5.  Jim has fun on the _____.

rise
ripe
ride

6.  He rides home on his _____.

take
bike
bite

 THINK! **Why do you think Jim chose the ride?**

Say the name of each picture. Print the missing vowels on the line. Trace the whole word.

1 r _ _ d

2 p _ g

3 d _ m _

4 f _ r

5 _ _ _ _

6 _ n h _ v _

7 l _ d

8 k _ t _

9 f _ v _

10 b _ k _

11 d _ v _

12 s _ x

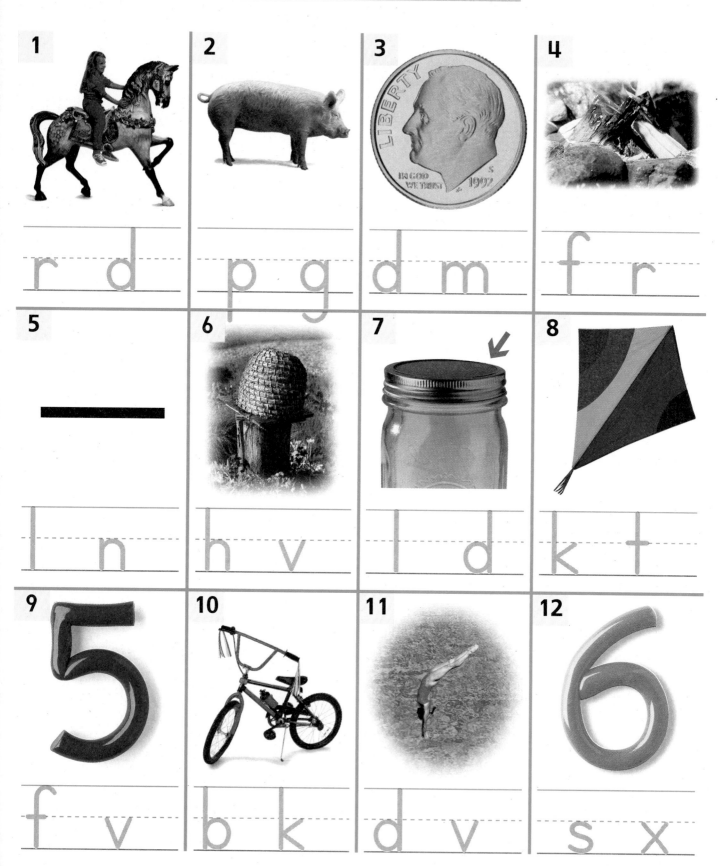

Lesson 84
Long vowel i: Spelling

 Home

 Point to several of the words your child wrote and ask him or her to read them.

Circle the word that will finish the sentence. Print it on the line.

1. Mike likes his _____.

bite
bike
bake

2. It has a nine on the _____.

side
sale
sand

3. It is the same size as _____.

miss
mine
mitt

4. Mike will _____ it in the race.

ride
ripe
rake

5. The race is six _____ long!

miss
mills
miles

6. Last time it ended in a _____.

tie
tide
tip

Why do you think Mike likes his bike?

Say the name of each picture. Print the picture name on the line. In the last box, draw a picture of a long **i** word. Print the picture name.

1. bike

2.

3.

4.

5.

6.

7.

8.

9.

10.

11.

12.

Lesson 85
Long vowel i: Spelling

 Home

Ask your child to read each word he or she wrote.

Read the story. Use long i words to finish the sentences.

Flying a Kite

Children everywhere like to fly kites.
In China, kites have shapes.
They look like snakes or bugs.

Children in Japan fly kites.
Kites fly high on special days.

Would you like to fly a kite?
Hold the line tight.
Make your kite sail.

_____

1. Children everywhere like to fly _____.

2. In Japan, kites fly _____ on special days.

3. Hold the _____ tight.

 **Why do you have to hold the line tight?**

Write about a kite you would like. Tell what it looks like. The words in the box may help you.

smile	like	nice
blue	fly	ride

Lesson 86
Review long vowel i: Writing

Home Ask your child to spell the words she or he wrote on page 179.

6

It is getting late.
Ty pulls in his line.

8

How do you think
Ty's mom will feel?

FOLD

FOLD

3

Ty rides his bike to High Pond.
He will catch a fish for his mom.

HIGH POND

1

This book belongs to:

TY'S LINE

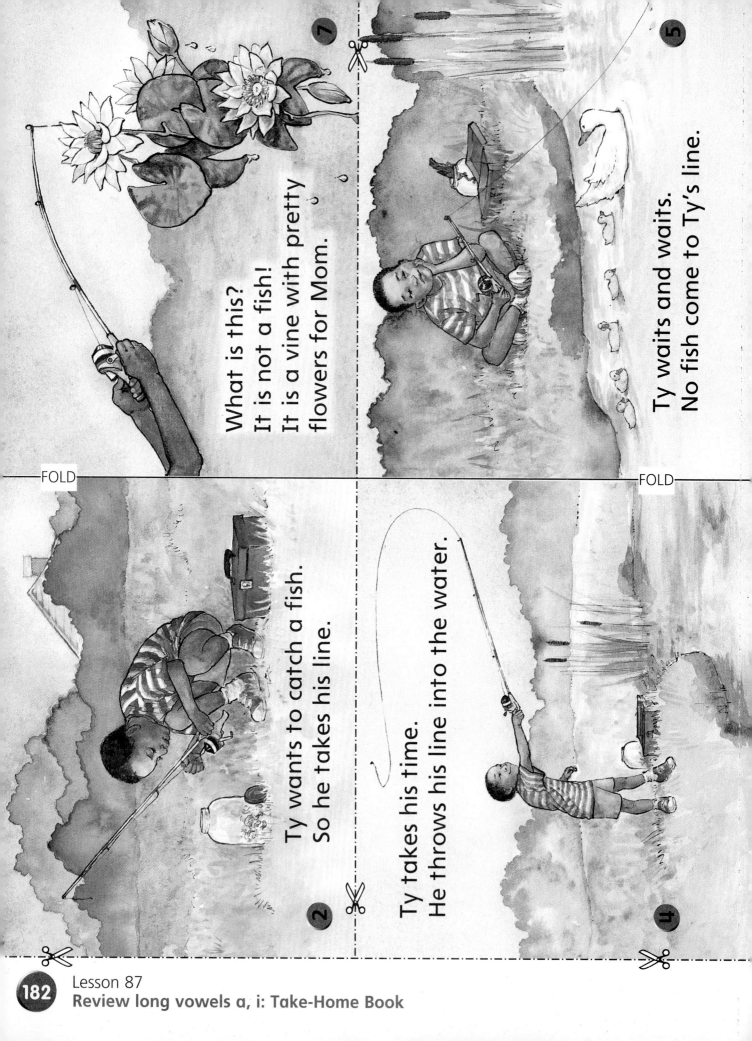

7

FOLD

What is this?
It is not a fish!
It is a vine with pretty flowers for Mom.

5

Ty waits and waits.
No fish come to Ty's line.

FOLD

Ty wants to catch a fish.
So he takes his line.

2

Ty takes his time.
He throws his line into the water.

4

Lesson 87
Review long vowels a, i: Take-Home Book

Lu used a tube
Of strong white glue
To paste her cube
On top of Sue's.

▶ **Tube** has the long sound of **u**. **Circle** each picture whose name has the long sound of **u**.

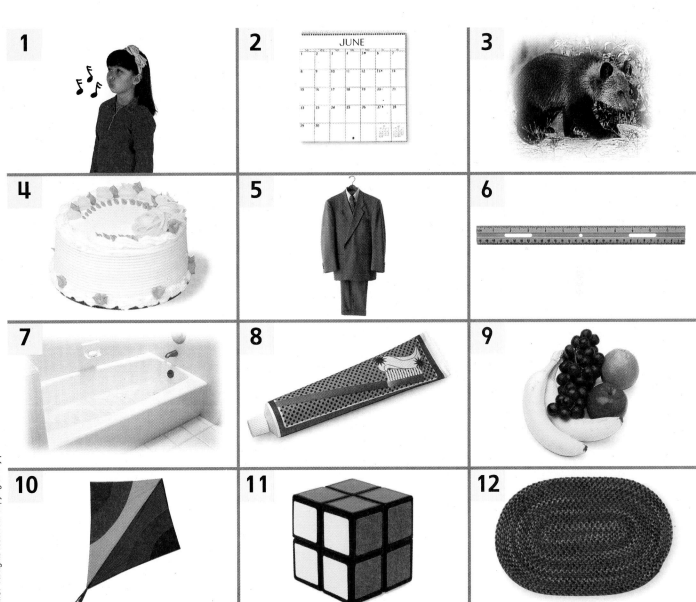

1	2 JUNE	3
4	5	6
7	8	9
10	11	12

Say the names of the pictures in each row.
Color the pictures whose names rhyme.

1

2

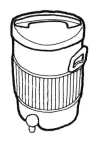   

3

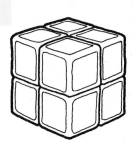   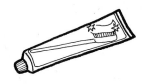

4

 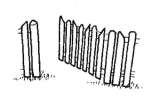  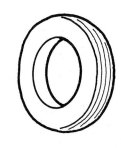

5

Lesson 88
Long vowel u: Phonograms

Ask your child to name the rhyming pictures and tell whether they have a long or short *u* sound.

184

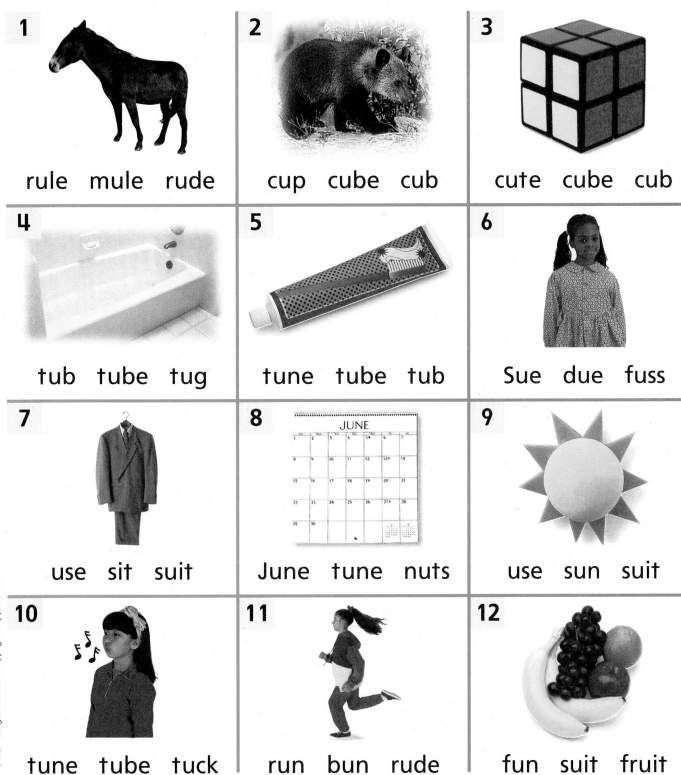

1	**2**	**3**
rule mule rude	cup cube cub	cute cube cub
4	**5**	**6**
tub tube tug	tune tube tub	Sue due fuss
7	**8**	**9**
use sit suit	June tune nuts	use sun suit
10	**11**	**12**
tune tube tuck	run bun rude	fun suit fruit

Read each sentence. **Use** the code to make each pair of words. **Print** them on the lines. Then **circle** the word that finishes the sentence.

1 = a	2 = e	3 = i	4 = u	5 = b	6 = c
7 = f	8 = l	9 = m	10 = r	11 = s	12 = t

1. June plays the

_____   _____.
12 4 5 1   10 4 8 2

2. Luke will feed his

_____   _____.
7 8 4 12 2   9 4 8 2

3. Sue likes to eat

_____   _____.
6 4 5 2   7 10 4 3 12

4. Ben got a new

_____   _____.
11 4 3 12   6 8 4 2

DUKE

5. Duke's house is

_____   _____.
12 10 4 2   5 8 4 2

Lesson 89
Long vowel u

Home

Ask your child to tell you how he or she figured out each missing word.

Say the name of each picture. If the vowel sound is short, color the box with the word short. If the vowel sound is long, color the box with the word long.

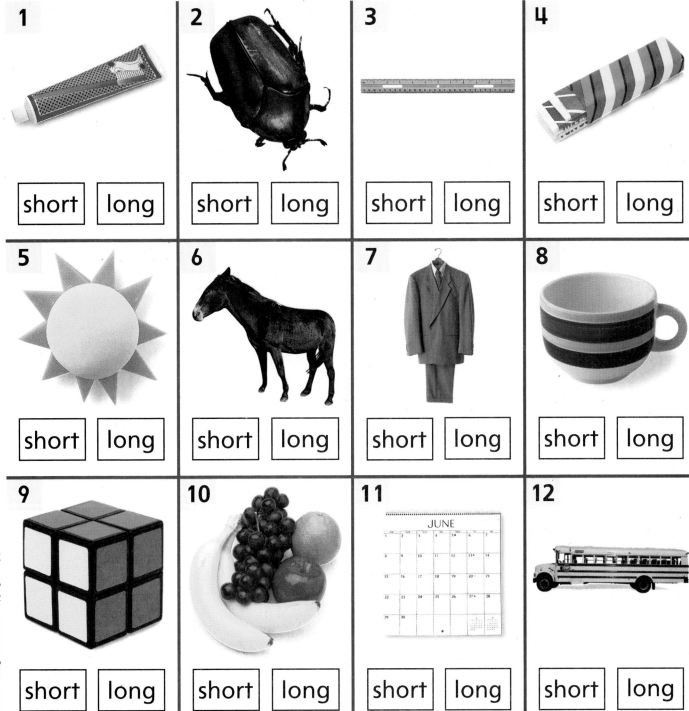

1
short long

2
short long

3
short long

4
short long

5
short long

6
short long

7
short long

8
short long

9
short long

10
short long

11
short long

12
short long

Color the bubble blue if it has three long **u** words in it.

1.
rude
Sue
use

2.
cub
tub
tube

3.
line
mine
nine

4.
suit
tune
cube

5.
mule
rule
tune

6.
fire
tire
ride

7.
glue
hut
June

8.
use
rule
Sue

9.
cute
mute
suit

10.
pail
sail
tail

11.
mile
file
pile

12.
due
clue
glue

13.
rug
tug
mug

Lesson 90
Long vowel u

Home

Have your child read the words in uncolored bubbles and name the vowel sounds.

Say the name of each picture. **Circle** its name.

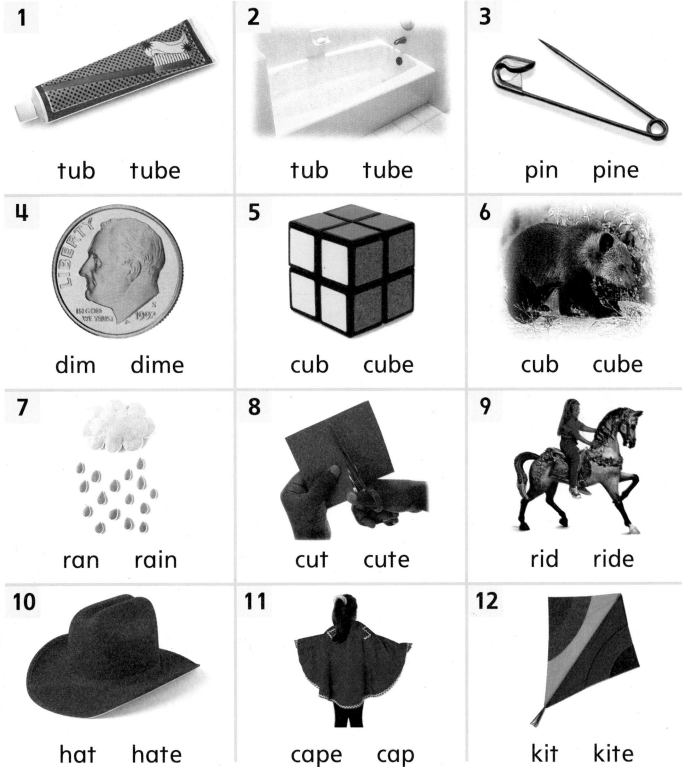

1 tub   tube

2 tub   tube

3 pin   pine

4 dim   dime

5 cub   cube

6 cub   cube

7 ran   rain

8 cut   cute

9 rid   ride

10 hat   hate

11 cape   cap

12 kit   kite

Lesson 91
Long vowel u: Picture-text match

189

Look at the picture. **Circle** the word that will finish the sentence. **Print** it on the line.

1. Luke has a _____.

   fox
   box
   ox

2. The box looks like a _____.

   cute
   cube
   cub

3. He got it from _____.

   rule
   Sue
   due

4. Luke has a _____ of glue in it.

   tune
   tub
   tube

5. He will put a _____ in it, too.

   ruler
   rude
   rubs

6. Luke will take it on the _____.

   suit
   bun
   bus

THINK! **Where do you think Luke is taking the box?**

Lesson 91
Long vowel u: Words in context

Ask your child to read all the words
with the long *u* sound.

Say the name of each picture. **Print** the missing vowels on the line. **Trace** the whole word.

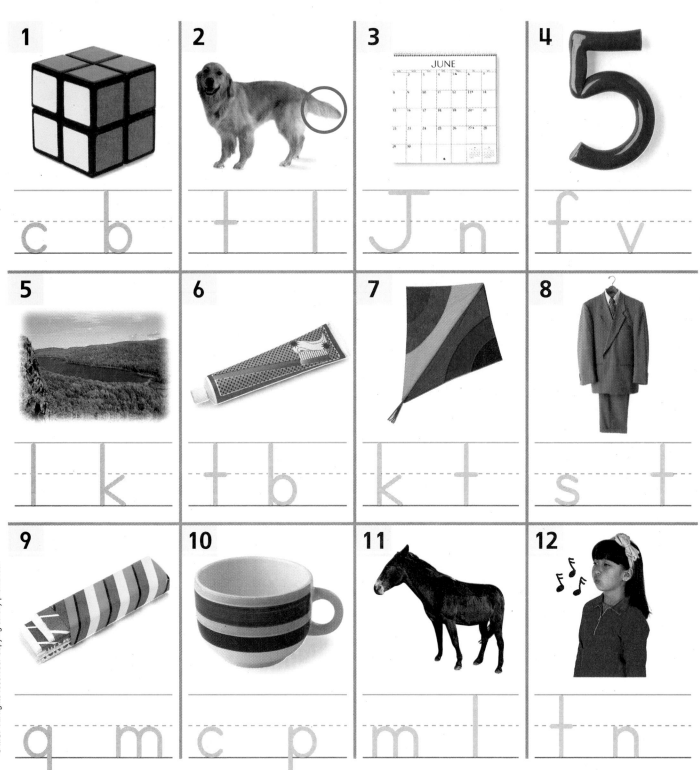

1

c _ _ b

2

t _ l

3

J _ n

4

f _ v _

5

l _ k _

6

t _ b _

7

k _ t _

8

s _ _ t

9

g _ _ m

10

c _ p

11

m _ l _

12

t _ n _

Circle the word that will finish the sentence. Print it on the line.

1. Sue has a _____.

   must
   mule
   mile

2. Is a mule a _____ pet?

   cute
   cube
   cut

3. Can a mule hum a _____?

   tub
   tug
   tune

4. Does it like to eat _____?

   fun
   fruit
   rule

5. I do not have a _____.

   cute
   clue
   cuts

6. You can ask _____.

   sun
   Sue
   suit

 **Where do you think Sue lives? Why?**

Lesson 92
Long vowel u: Words in context

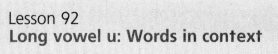 Read each sentence and ask your child to read the word he or she wrote.

Say the name of each picture. Print the picture name on the line. In the last box, draw a picture of a long **u** word. Print the picture name.

1

cube

2

3

4

5

6

7

8

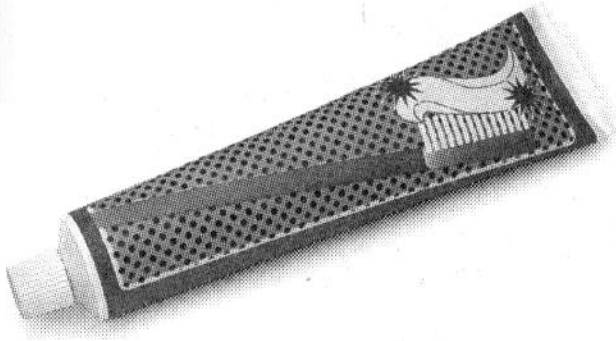

9

10

11

12

► **Circle the long a, long i, and long u words in the puzzle.**

r	a	i	n
s	u	i	t
r	a	c	a
t	i	e	p
m	u	l	e

rain ice tape
suit tie mule

► **Print the word from the box that names each picture.**

1.  rain

2.

3.

4.

5.

6.

Lesson 93
Review long vowels a, i, u

Home   Ask your child to use three of the words in the box in sentences.

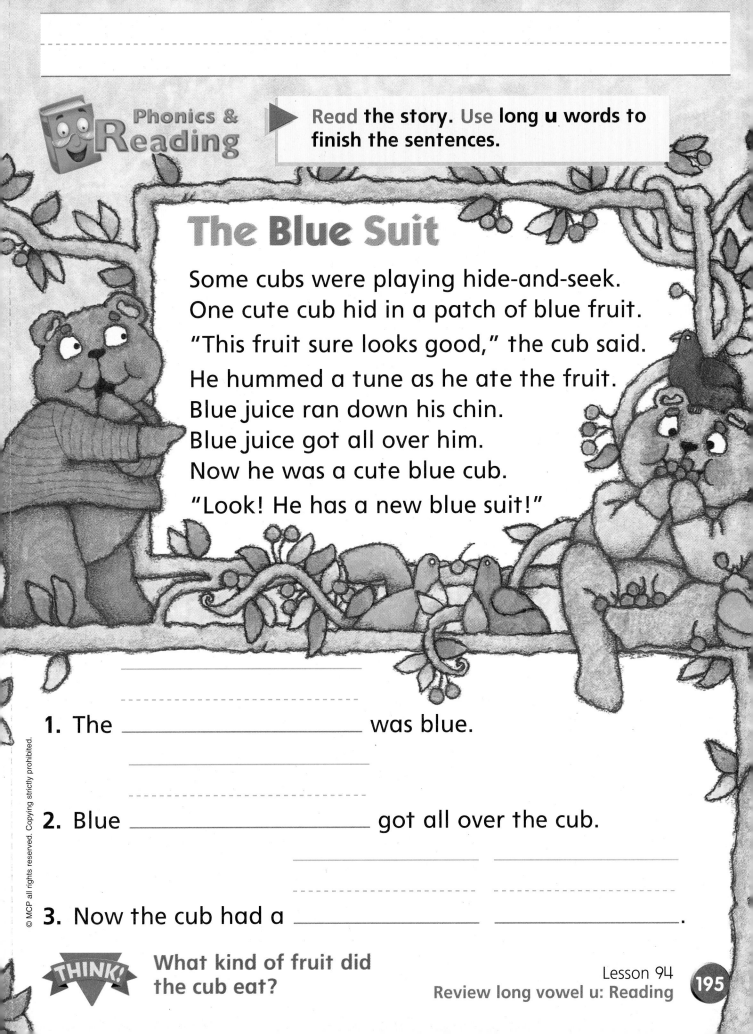

Phonics & Reading

▶ Read **the story**. Use **long u** words to finish the sentences.

The Blue Suit

Some cubs were playing hide-and-seek.
One cute cub hid in a patch of blue fruit.

"This fruit sure looks good," the cub said.

He hummed a tune as he ate the fruit.
Blue juice ran down his chin.
Blue juice got all over him.
Now he was a cute blue cub.

"Look! He has a new blue suit!"

1. The _____ was blue.

2. Blue _____ got all over the cub.

3. Now the cub had a _____ _____.

THINK! What kind of fruit did the cub eat?

Phonics & Writing

Write a story about something silly that happened to you. Read your story to the class. The words in the box may help you.

use	huge	rule
suit	cube	fruit

Lesson 94
Review long vowel u: Writing

Home

Help your child think of a title for the story.

6

Make a bird like this. Move your hands and the bird will fly.

✄ **8**

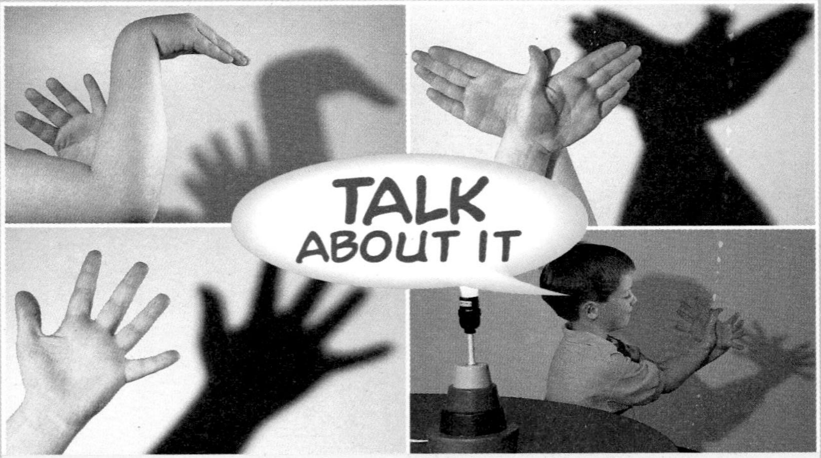

How can you make the shadow pictures bigger? Smaller?

TALK ABOUT IT

---FOLD---

Hold your hands up to a white space. Let a light shine on them.

3

---FOLD---

This book belongs to:

_____

HAND GAMES

✄ **1**

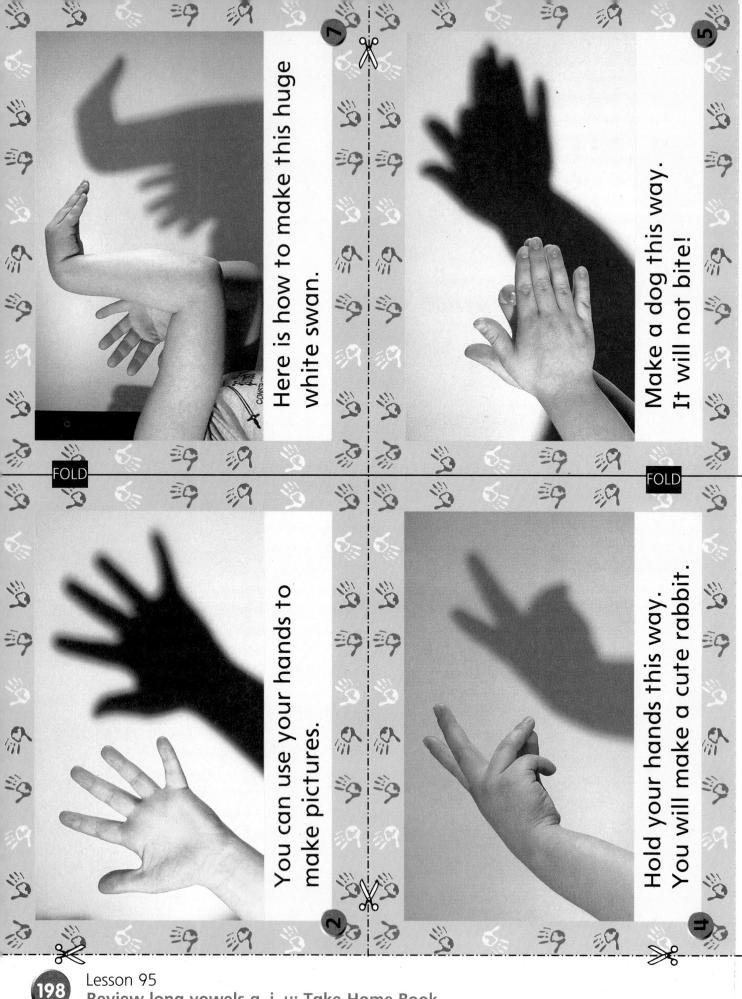

Here is how to make this huge white swan.

7

Make a dog this way. It will not bite!

5

You can use your hands to make pictures.

2

Hold your hands this way. You will make a cute rabbit.

4

FOLD

FOLD

Lesson 95
Review long vowels a, i, u: Take-Home Book

Turn that jump rope,
High, low, fast, slow!
Ready! Set!
Come on, let's go!

▶ Rope **has the long sound of o.** Circle **each picture whose name has the long sound of o.**

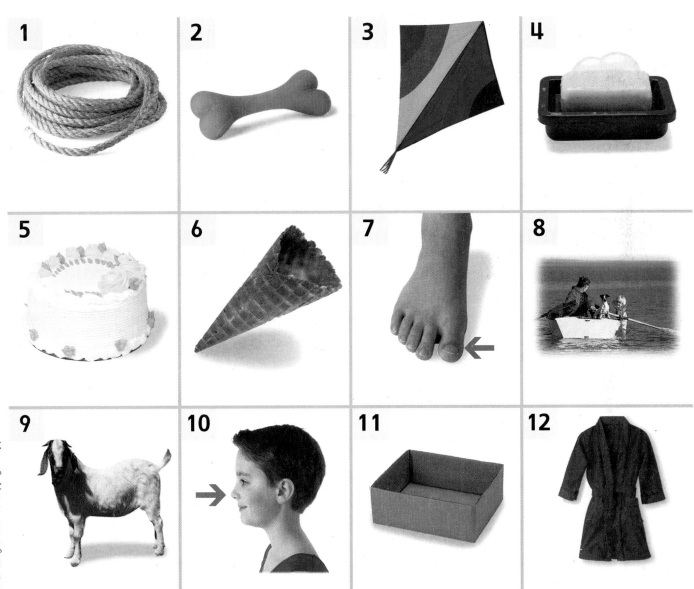

1	**2**	**3**	**4**
5	**6**	**7**	**8**
9	**10**	**11**	**12**

Say the names of the pictures in each circle. Color the parts of the circle that have pictures with long **o** names.

1.
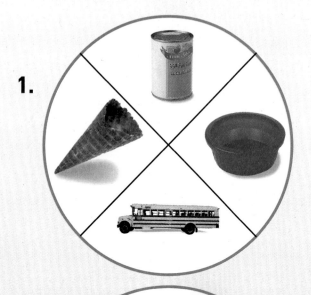

2.
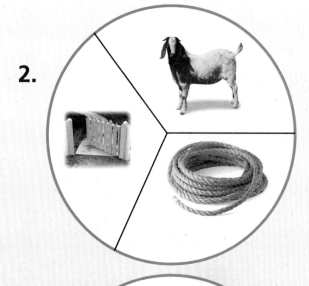

3.

4.

5.
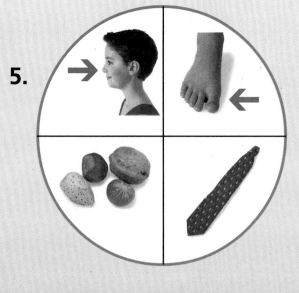

6.

Lesson 96
Long vowel o: Phonemic awareness

 Ask your child to name each picture that has a long o vowel sound.

Say the names of the pictures in each row.
Color the pictures whose names rhyme.

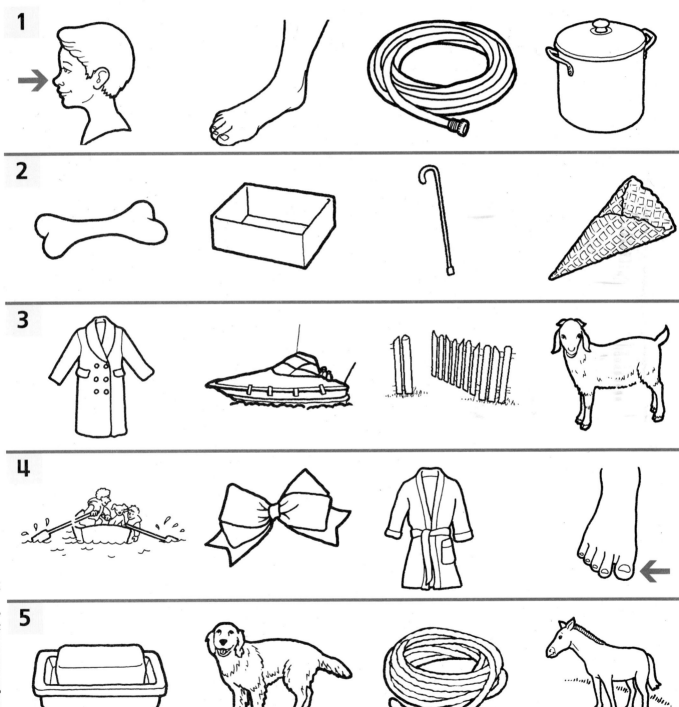

1

2

3

4

5

Lesson 97
Long vowel o: Phonograms

201

Say the name of each picture. Circle its name.

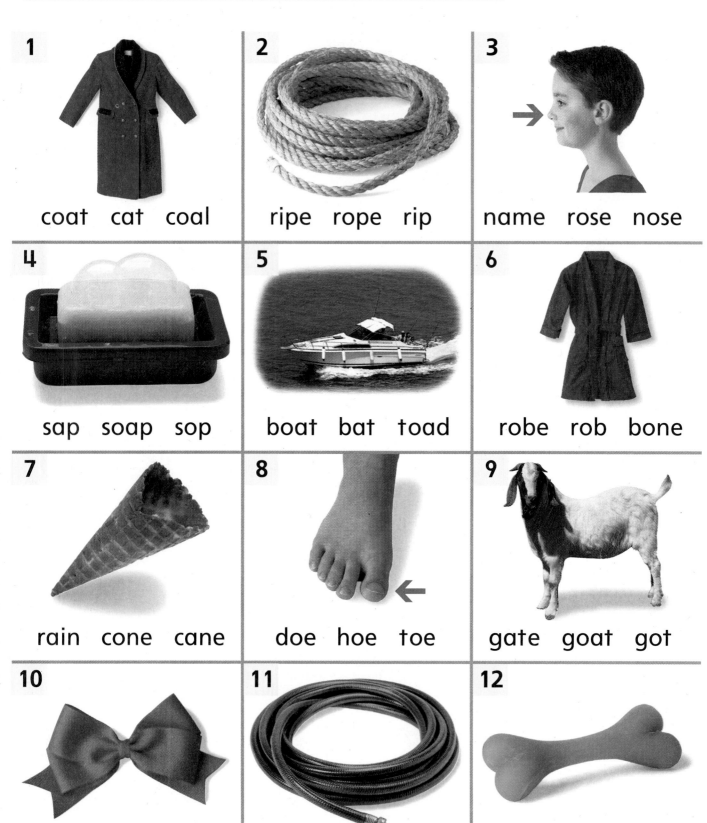

1
coat   cat   coal

2
ripe   rope   rip

3
name   rose   nose

4
sap   soap   sop

5
boat   bat   toad

6
robe   rob   bone

7
rain   cone   cane

8
doe   hoe   toe

9
gate   goat   got

10
row   bow   toe

11
hose   hope   hot

12
cone   boat   bone

Ask your child to tell which words on the page rhyme.

Say the name of each picture. **Circle** the letters that make the long sound of **o**.

1. g o a t

2. b o w

3. n o s e

4. c o n e

5. r o p e

6. b o a t

7. n o t e

8. r o w

9. s o a p

10. h o s e

11. c o a t

12. b o n e

Look at the picture. Then **follow** the directions below.

Directions

1. Color the hose green.
2. Color the boat blue.
3. Circle the girl who will row.
4. Draw a toad on the stone.

5. Make an X on the hoe.
6. Color the roses red.
7. Draw a hole for the mole.
8. Draw a rope on the goat.

Home

Point to long o words and ask your child to tell which letters spell the vowel sound.

Say the name of each picture. If the vowel sound is short, color the box with the word short. If the vowel sound is long, color the box with the word long.

1 short | long

2 short | long

3 short | long

4 short | long

5 short | long

6 short | long

7 short | long

8 short | long

9 short | long

10 short | long

11 short | long

12 short | long

Say the name of each picture. Circle the words in the boxes that rhyme with the picture name.

1

bone	cane	loan	moan	can
Joan	tone	run	zone	coat

2

got	boat	coat	note	vote
rate	cute	tote	gate	moat

3

snow	doe	tip	top	slow
go	tube	row	foe	tail

4

rope	slow	blow	rip	snow
low	ride	bow	tow	rock

Lesson 99
Long vowel o: Phonemic awareness

Ask your child to read the words in each row and to name the vowel sound.

▶ **Say the name of each picture. Circle its name.**

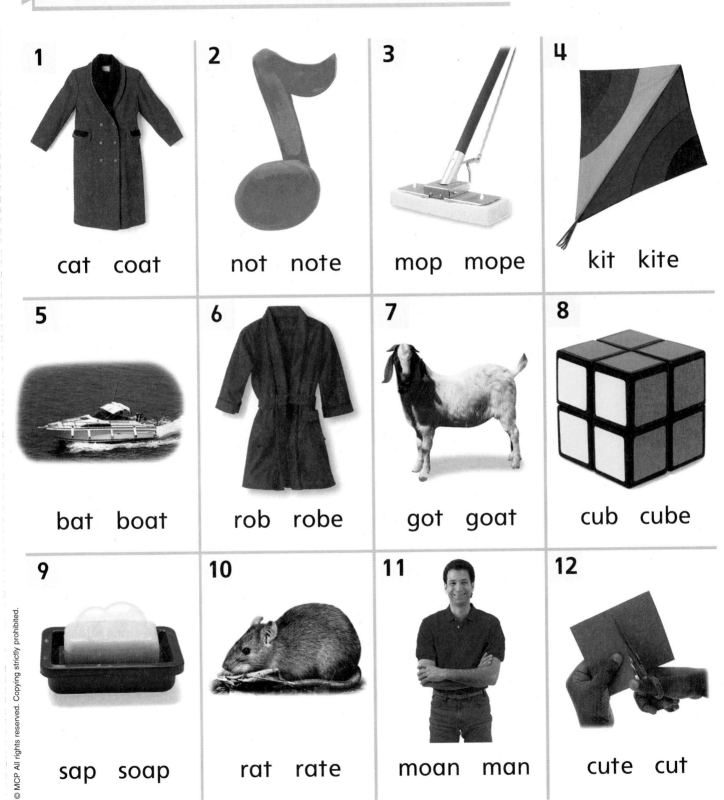

1. cat coat

2. not note

3. mop mope

4. kit kite

5. bat boat

6. rob robe

7. got goat

8. cub cube

9. sap soap

10. rat rate

11. moan man

12. cute cut

Look at the picture. **Circle** the word that will finish the sentence. **Print** it on the line.

1. A mole hides in a _____.

hose
hole
hope

2. A fish swims in a _____.

box
bone
bowl

3. A goat eats a _____.

bone
cone
cane

4. A cat goes up a _____.

poke
pole
loan

5. A dog begs for a _____.

bone
robe
boat

6. A fox cleans its _____.

cone
coal
coat

THINK! Which animals make good pets?

Lesson 100
Long vowel o: Words in context

 Home

Point to the name of each animal and ask your child to identify the vowel sound.

Say the name of each picture. Print the missing vowels on the line. Trace the whole word.

1 c __ n

2 h __ s __

3 r __ b __

4 t __ p

5 r __ p __

6 c __ t

7 n __ t __

8 n __ s __

9 s __ p

10 p __ t

11 m __ p

12 b __ t

**Circle the word that will finish the sentence.
Print it on the line.**

1. The store is up the _____.

road
robe
role

2. Joan goes in and smells the _____.

song
soak
soap

3. It gets on her _____.

not
nose
hope

4. Joan sees a red _____.

boss
bow
row

5. She sees a blue _____, too.

robe
rob
ripe

6. She will pay and take them _____.

hose
hole
home

THINK! What could Joan do with the bow?

Lesson 101
Long vowel o: Words in context

Home

Ask your child to read the completed sentences.

Say the name of each picture. Print the picture name on the line. In the last box, draw a picture of a long **o** word. Print the picture name.

1

bone

2

3

4

5

6

7

8

9

10

11

12

Lesson 102
Long vowel o: Spelling

211

Say each picture name. Draw a line through the three pictures in a row that have the same long vowel sound.

1

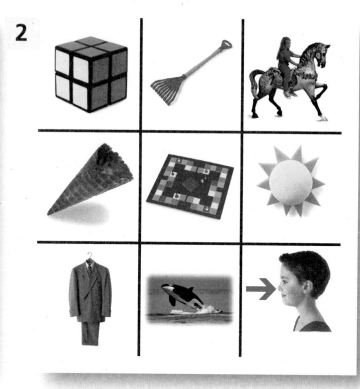

2

3

4

Lesson 102
Review: Long vowels a, i, u, o

Home

Ask your child to tell which long vowel "won" in each puzzle.

Read **the story.** Use **long o words to finish the sentences.**

Joe's Show

Joe wanted to put on a show.
Joe's friend Rose came over.
Both children hoped the show would go well.

Oh, no!
Joe's dog Pogo poked her nose in.
"Go away, Pogo!"
Everyone thought the show was a good joke.

1. Joe wanted to put on a _____.

2. Pogo _____ her nose in.

3. Everyone thought the _____ was a good _____.

 **THINK!** **Why do you think everyone is laughing?**

▶ **Pretend you are having a show. Write a sign that tells about your show. The words in the box may help you.**

show	over
go	o'clock
open	hope

_____

- -

_____

- -

_____

- -

_____

- -

_____

- -

_____

Help your child think of a name for his or her show.

6

Do you like to play clapping games?
Many children in Turkey do.

8

Which game that is played in
other places do you like best?

TALK ABOUT IT

3

In some places children like
to play games with string.
These children are playing
a tug-of-war game.

1

This book belongs to:

_____

Games Around The Globe

Review long vowels a, i, u, o: Take-Home Book

Soccer is a game that children in Mexico play. Children in many other places also like soccer.

7

This game with two ropes is called Double Dutch. Dutch children started this game.

5

FOLD

FOLD

Children around the globe like to play.

2

Children in many places like to jump rope.

4

Way up in a tree
Is a neat place to be.
From up here I can see,
But the green leaves hide me!

▶ **Tree has the long sound of e. Circle each picture whose name has the long sound of e.**

1

2

3

4

5

6

7

8

9

10

11

12

Say the names of the pictures in each row. Color the pictures whose names rhyme.

1

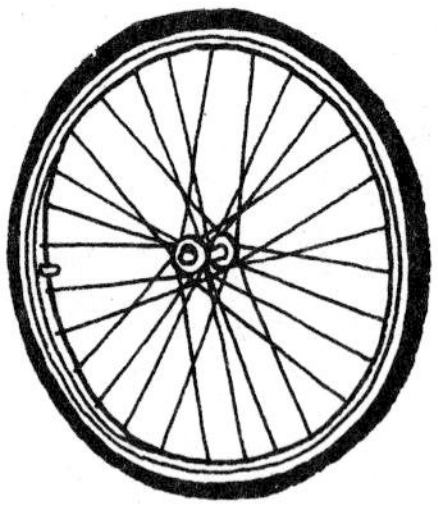 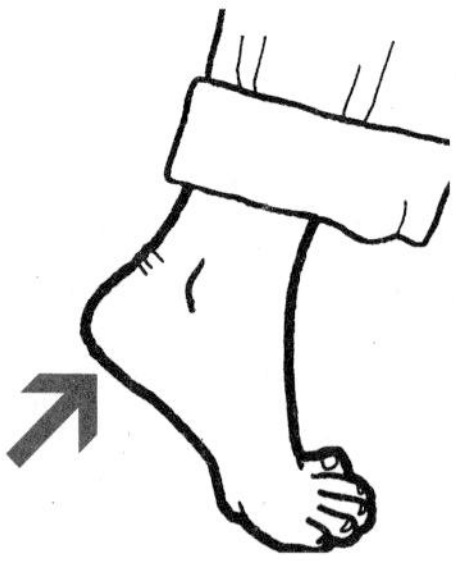 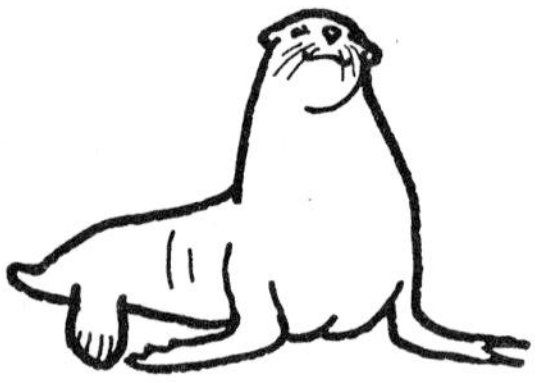 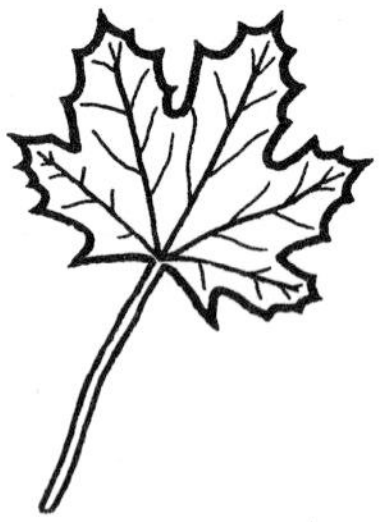

2

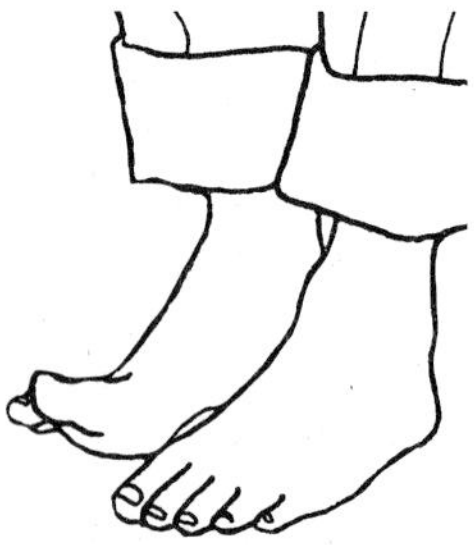 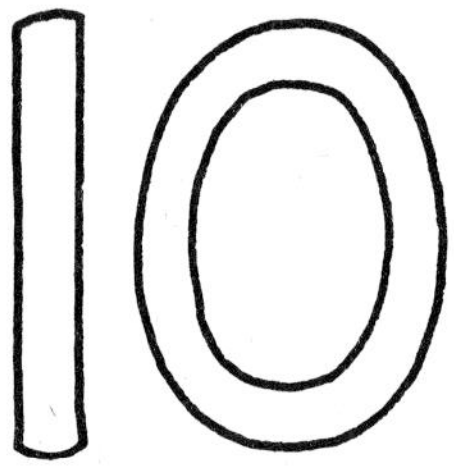 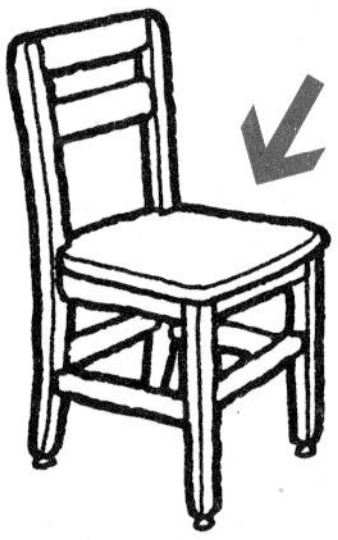 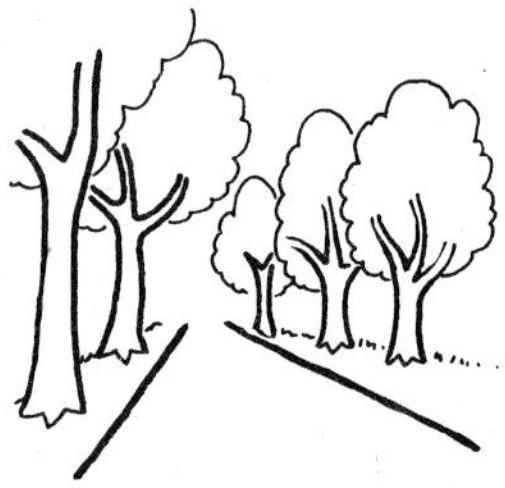

3

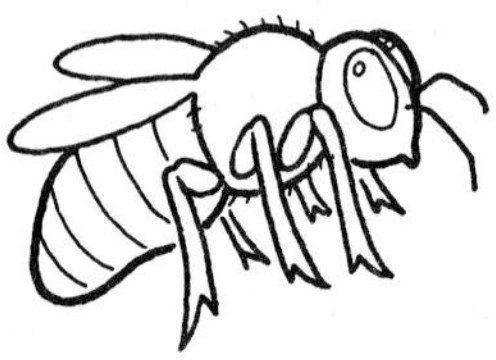 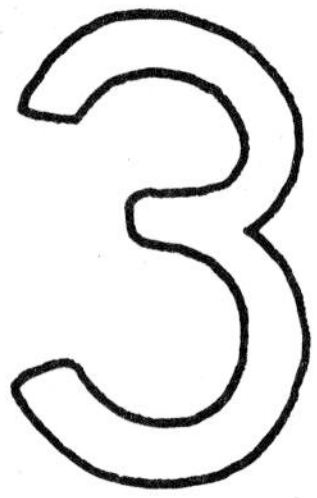 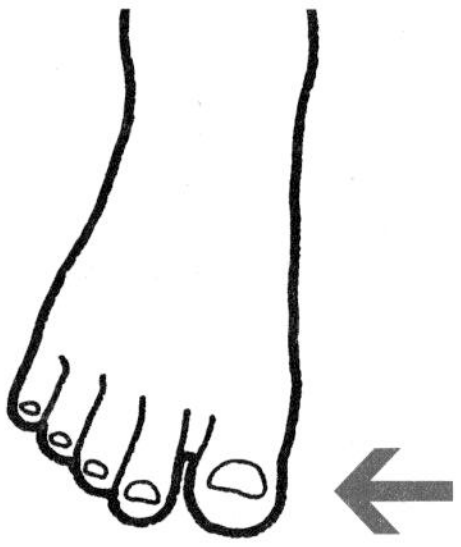 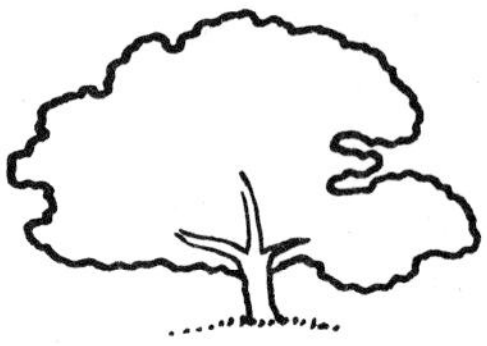

4

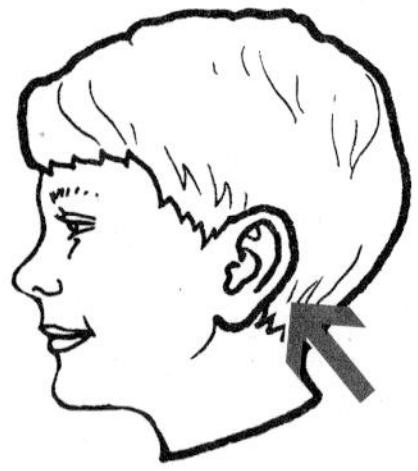 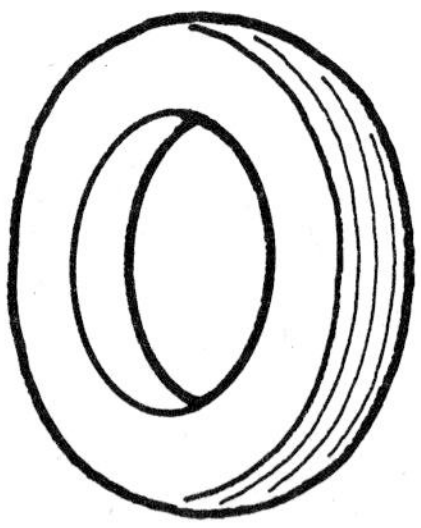 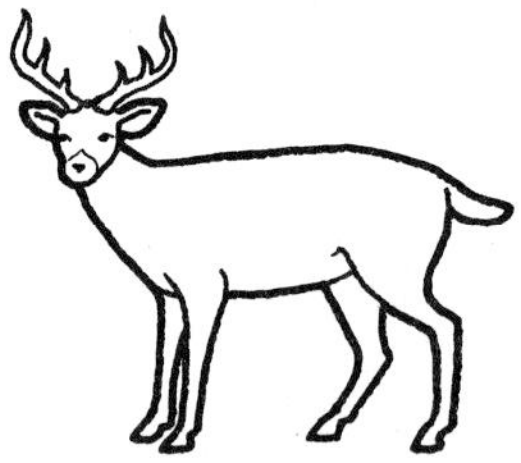 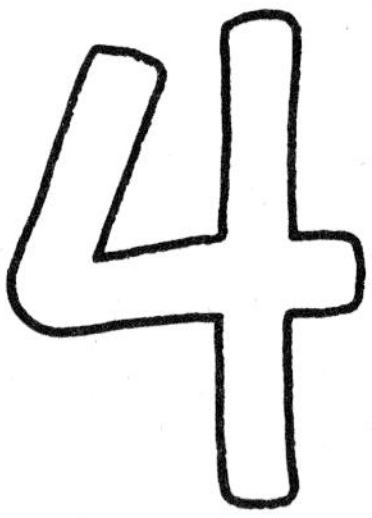

5

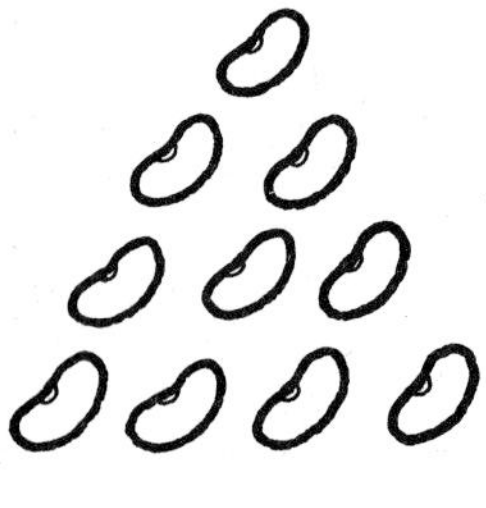 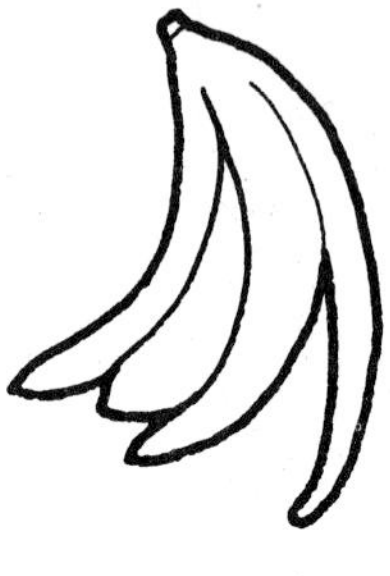 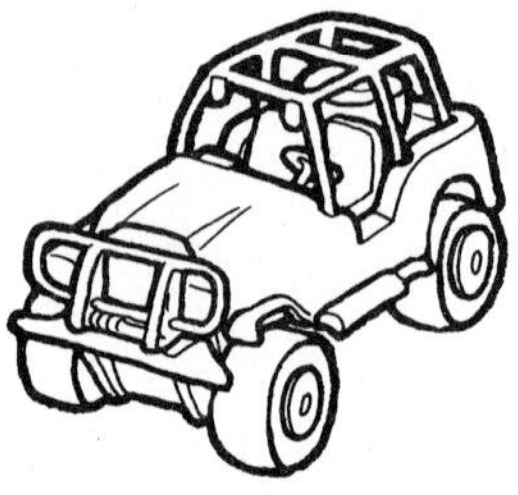 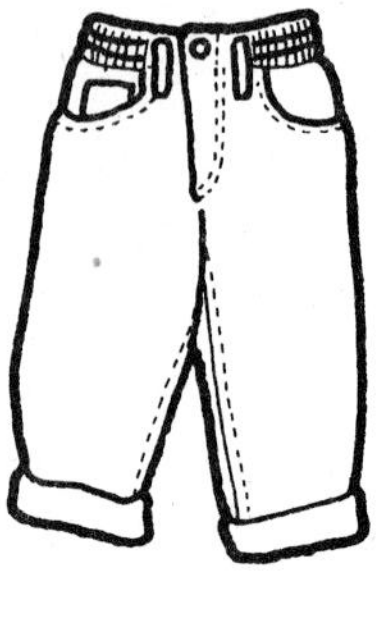

Home: Ask your child to name the vowel sounds in the names of the uncolored pictures.

Say the name of each picture. Circle its name.

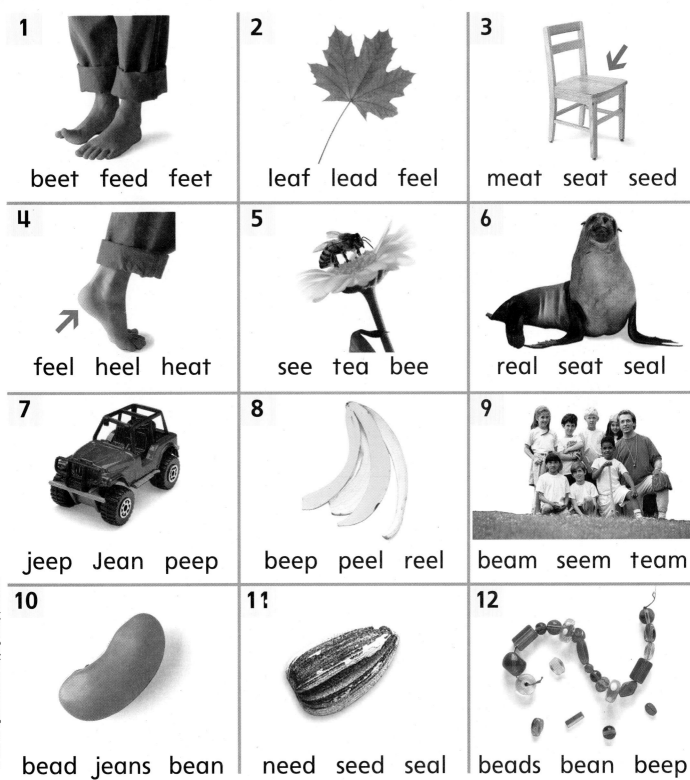

1. beet   feed   feet

2. leaf   lead   feel

3. meat   seat   seed

4. feel   heel   heat

5. see   tea   bee

6. real   seat   seal

7. jeep   Jean   peep

8. beep   peel   reel

9. beam   seem   team

10. bead   jeans   bean

11. need   seed   seal

12. beads   bean   beep

Help Jean and Lee get to the Jelly Bean Shop. Read each word. Draw a line to join the long e words.

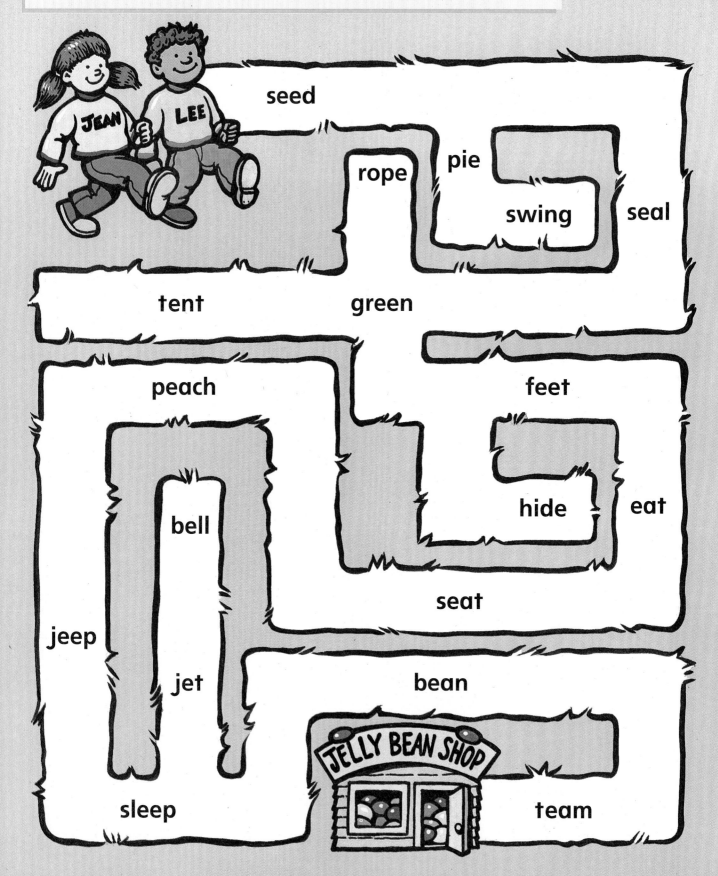

seed

pie

rope

swing

seal

tent

green

peach

feet

bell

hide

eat

jeep

seat

jet

bean

sleep

JELLY BEAN SHOP

team

Home

Ask your child to read the long *e* words along the path to the Jelly Bean Shop.

Say the name of each picture. If the vowel sound is short, color the box with the word short. If the vowel sound is long, color the box with the word long.

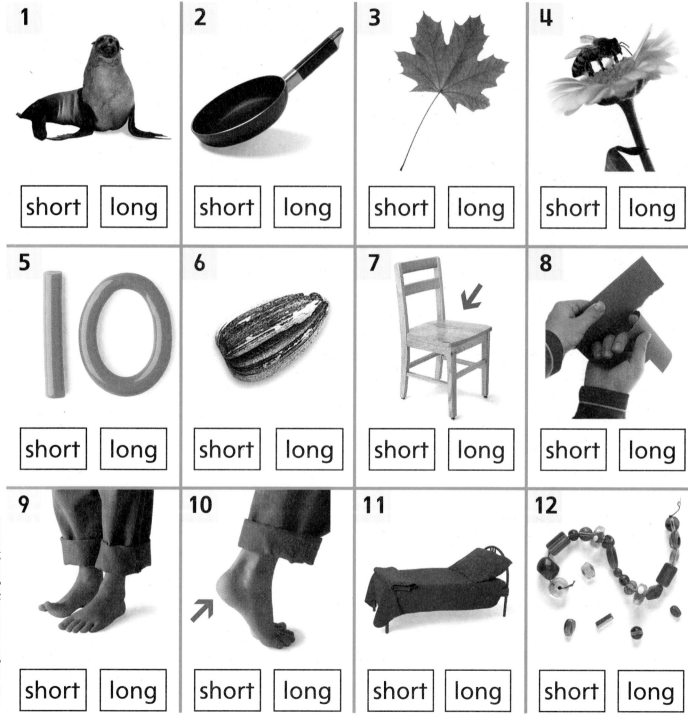

1 | short | long

2 | short | long

3 | short | long

4 | short | long

5 | short | long

6 | short | long

7 | short | long

8 | short | long

9 | short | long

10 | short | long

11 | short | long

12 | short | long

Say the name of each picture. **Circle** the words in the boxes that rhyme with the picture name.

1

me	team	see	met	bean
he	we	fee	tea	seed

2

feel	seal	sell	deep	deal
men	meal	real	leaf	help

3

feet	beat	bet	heat	set
seat	net	neat	peat	wet

4

please	pegs	feet	meats	fleas
seals	teas	begs	deep	team

Lesson 107
Long vowel e

 Ask your child whether the vowel sound in some of the words is long or short.

Say the name of each picture. Circle its name.

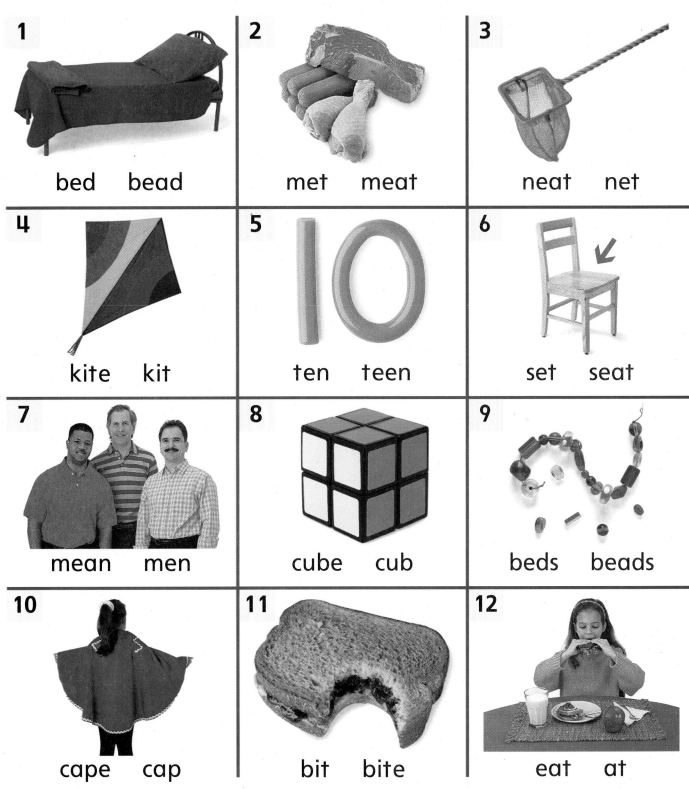

1. bed   bead

2. met   meat

3. neat   net

4. kite   kit

5. ten   teen

6. set   seat

7. mean   men

8. cube   cub

9. beds   beads

10. cape   cap

11. bit   bite

12. eat   at

1. I sit in my _____.

seal
seed
seat

2. It feels nice to rest my _____.

feet
feel
feed

3. Dean heats up the _____.

met
team
meat

4. Mom piles on the _____.

peak
peas
pens

5. Can I eat a heap of _____?

beds
beans
beads

6. After I eat I brush my _____.

teeth
team
ten

 **What is your favorite food?**

Say the name of each picture. **Print** the missing vowels on the line. **Trace** the whole word.

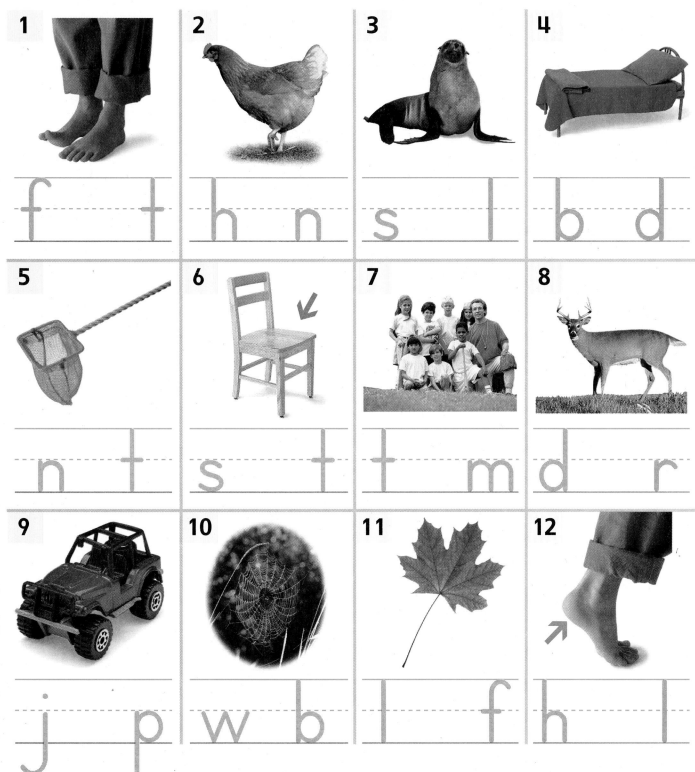

1. f _ _ t

2. h _ n s

3. s _ _ l

4. b _ d

5. n _ t

6. s _ _ t

7. t _ _ m

8. d _ _ r

9. j _ _ p

10. w _ b

11. l _ _ f

12. h _ _ l

Circle the word that will finish the sentence. **Print** it on the line.

1. We rode to Lee's game in the ———————.

jeans
jeep
peep

2. We sat in a row of ———————.

seats
seals
seems

3. The Seals beat the Bees last ———————.

well
week
keep

4. The Bees are in the ———————.

lead
leap
leak

5. The Seals ——————— to win.

neat
need
seed

6. Will Lee's ——————— win the game?

tent
tame
team

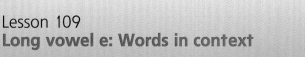 **Which team do you think will win?**

Lesson 109
Long vowel e: Words in context

 Home Read the sentences with your child.

Say the name of each picture. **Print** the picture name on the line. In the last box, **draw** a picture of a long e word. **Print** the picture name.

1

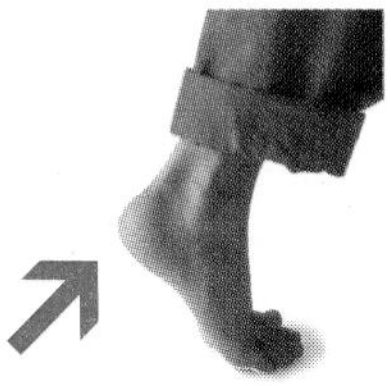

heel

2

3

4

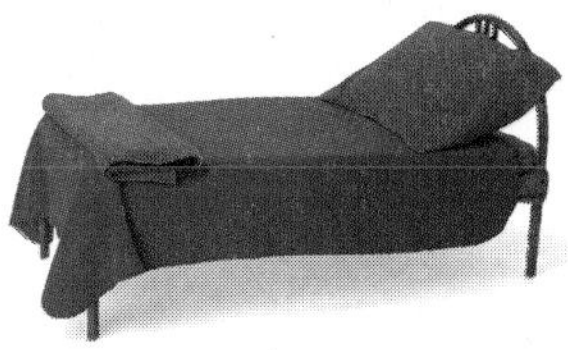

5

6

7

8

9

10

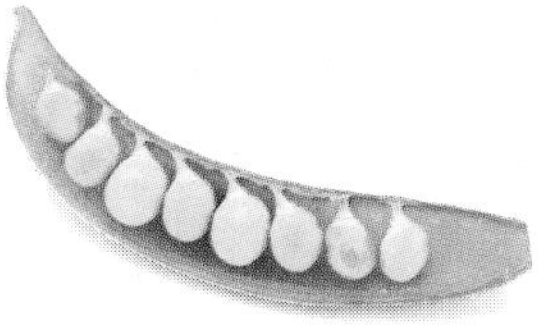

11

12

Look at the vowel sound. Color the pictures in each row whose names have that vowel sound.

1 Long a				
2 Long i				
3 Long u	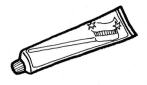			
4 Long o				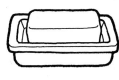
5 Long e	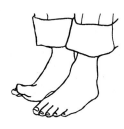		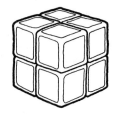	

Lesson 110
Review long vowels a, i, u, o, e

 Home

Ask your child to name the vowel sounds in the pictures they didn't color.

Blend the letter sounds together as you say each word. Then color the picture it names.

1 c a n e →

2 h o s e →

3 t u b →

4 s e a t →

5 p i n →

6 d o g →

Lesson 111
Review long and short a, i, u, o, e: Blending

229

1

c u b

2

m e a t

3

r a i n

4

p i g

5

m o p

6

t u b e

 Home Point to a picture and ask your child to read the word that matches it.

Say the name of each picture. Print the missing vowels on the lines. Trace the whole word.

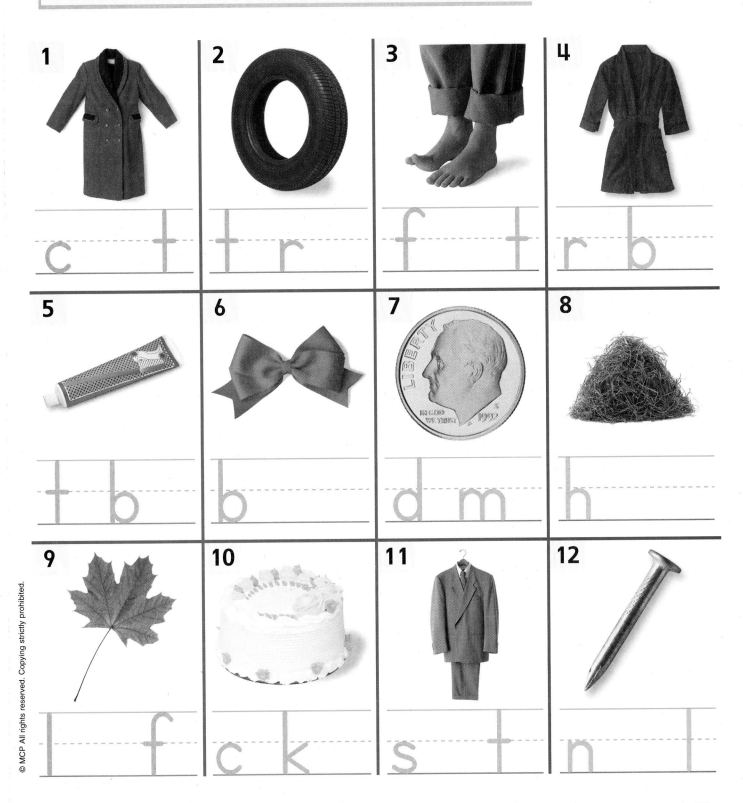

1 c _ _ t

2 t _ r _

3 f _ _ t

4 r _ b _

5 t _ b _

6 b _ _

7 d _ m _

8 h _ _

9 l _ _ f

10 c _ k _

11 s _ _ t

12 n _ _ l

Lesson 112
Review long vowels: Spelling

231

Read the word in the box. **Add** an e to make a long vowel word. **Write** it on the first line. Then **change** the vowel of the word in the box to make a short vowel word. **Write** it on the second line.

Long Vowel   **Short Vowel**

#	Box	Long Vowel	Short Vowel
1	tap	tape	top
2	pin		
3	cut		
4	hop		
5	not		
6	pan		
7	hid		

Home

Ask your child to read the words he or she wrote.

Phonics & Spelling

Say and spell each long vowel word. Print each word on a line in the box that shows its long vowel sound.

Word List

fruit	rain	pie	bean	bike
bone	hay	soap	seal	glue

Long a

_____ _____

Long i

_____ _____

Long u

_____ _____

Long o

_____ _____

Long e

_____ _____

Phonics & Writing

▶ Write a letter to a friend. Tell about a game, sport, or hobby you like. The words in the box may help you.

kite	rope	feet
bike	flute	day

Dear _____,

_____

_____

_____

_____

_____

Your friend,

_____

Book Corner

The Bike That Spike Likes
by Bill Kirk

Learn all about the bike that Spike likes.

 Home You may want to help your child address an envelope and mail the letter to a friend.

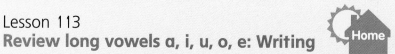

Do you think Bea will get to sleep?

8

Soon she was tangled up in the sheet,

6

This book belongs to:

No Sleep

FOLD

FOLD

A car made a very, very loud BEEP!

1

3

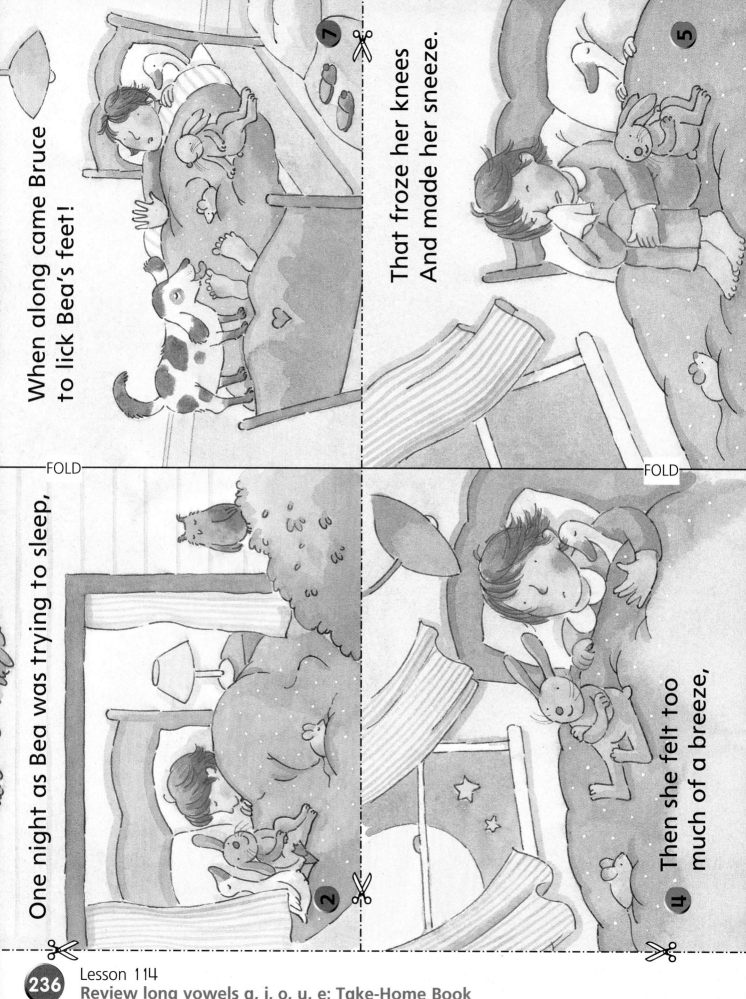

When along came Bruce
to lick Bea's feet!

7

That froze her knees
And made her sneeze.

5

FOLD

FOLD

One night as Bea was trying to sleep,

2

Then she felt too
much of a breeze,

4

Lesson 114
Review long vowels a, i, o, u, e: Take-Home Book

UNIT 3 CHECKUP

Say the name of each picture. Fill in the bubble beside the picture name.

1
- ○ cake
- ○ rake
- ○ coat
- ○ keep

2
- ○ mile
- ○ mail
- ○ ruler
- ○ mule

3
- ○ wave
- ○ vase
- ○ five
- ○ dive

4
- ○ bone
- ○ cone
- ○ cane
- ○ tune

5
- ○ jeans
- ○ jeep
- ○ deep
- ○ game

6
- ○ sail
- ○ seem
- ○ rose
- ○ suit

7
- ○ tie
- ○ toe
- ○ lie
- ○ tire

8
- ○ rail
- ○ road
- ○ read
- ○ rain

9
- ○ bait
- ○ goat
- ○ boat
- ○ toad

10
- ○ tile
- ○ tube
- ○ tape
- ○ time

11
- ○ mate
- ○ moat
- ○ boat
- ○ meat

12
- ○ rope
- ○ soap
- ○ pole
- ○ robe

Circle **the word that will finish the** sentence. Print **it on the line.**

1. Sue has a _____ blue kite.

net
neat

2. The kite does _____ have a tail yet.

not
note

3. Joe _____ up rags to make a tail.

cuts
cute

4. Then they sail the _____.

kit
kite

5. Sue hopes it does not _____.

ran
rain

6. The kite is stuck in a _____ tree!

pine
pin

UNIT 4

Consonant Blends

Theme: Everybody Eats

Read Along

The Pancake

Mix a pancake,
Stir a pancake,
Pop it in the pan;
Fry the pancake,
Toss the pancake—
Catch it if you can.

Christina Rossetti

▶ **Tell what you would do first, next, and last to make a pancake.**

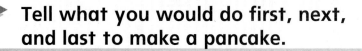

THINK! **What is your favorite food to make? How do you make it?**

Home Letter

Dear Family,

We are beginning to read and write words that begin and end with consonant blends and words with *y* as a vowel, such as the following.

gr	pl	str	lk	y

grapes   **plum**   **strawberry**   **milk**   **cherry**

As you can see, many food names begin or end with consonant blends or end with *y* as a vowel. In this unit, we will also be learning about food, nutrition, and health.

At-Home Activities

Here are some activities you and your child might like to do together.

▶ Make a grocery list. Ask your child to help you divide the items on the list into groups. Some groups might be frozen foods, dairy products, fresh fruits and vegetables, snacks, and drinks.

▶ Make a collage of favorite foods. Look through supermarket flyers. Point to various food items pictured and ask your child to name them. Challenge your child to spell the picture names or to tell what letter the names begin and end with.

You and your child might enjoy reading these books together.

Outside and Inside You
by Sandra Markle

A colorful photo essay reveals inner views of the human body.

Science Fun with Peanuts and Popcorn
by Rose Wyler

These science experiments help children learn about the properties of two foods: peanuts and popcorn.

Sincerely,

I love to munch
Fresh fruit for brunch
And have a bunch
Of grapes with lunch.

▶ **Say** the name of the first picture in each row.
Circle each picture in the row whose name begins
with the same blend.

1 grapes

2 tree

3 brush

4 crib

Say the name of the first picture in the row.
Color each picture in the row whose name begins
with the same blend.

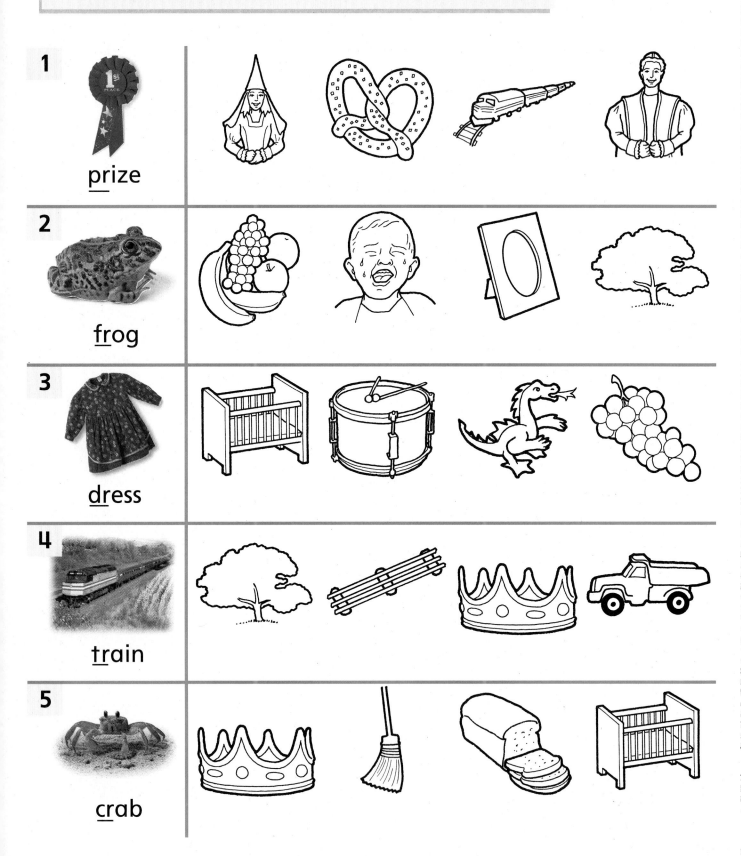

1 prize

2 frog

3 dress

4 train

5 crab

Lesson 116
R blends: Sound/letter correspondence

 Home

Ask your child to say the name
of each picture and spell the
first two letters of each word.

Say the name of each picture. Circle its name.

1 free tree	**2** trick brick	**3** prize cries
4 frog frame	**5** crab crib	**6** drive dress
7 braid bride	**8** grapes grass	**9** crane crown
10 drum drip	**11** frown frame	**12** grass grab

Say the name of each picture. **Print** its beginning blend on the line. **Trace** the whole word.

1	2	3
crab	ain	ide

4	5	6
uit	ick	ess

7	8	9
ize	ane	ee

10	11	12
um	ass	og

Lesson 117
R blends: Spelling

 Home

Point to a picture and ask your child to spell the word.

Slice the plum.
Plop it on a plate.
You take some.
I'll be glad to wait.

 Say the name of the first picture in the row.
Circle each picture in the row whose name begins with the same blend.

1 plug

2 block

3 club

4 flag

5 glass

Say the name of each picture. Circle its name.

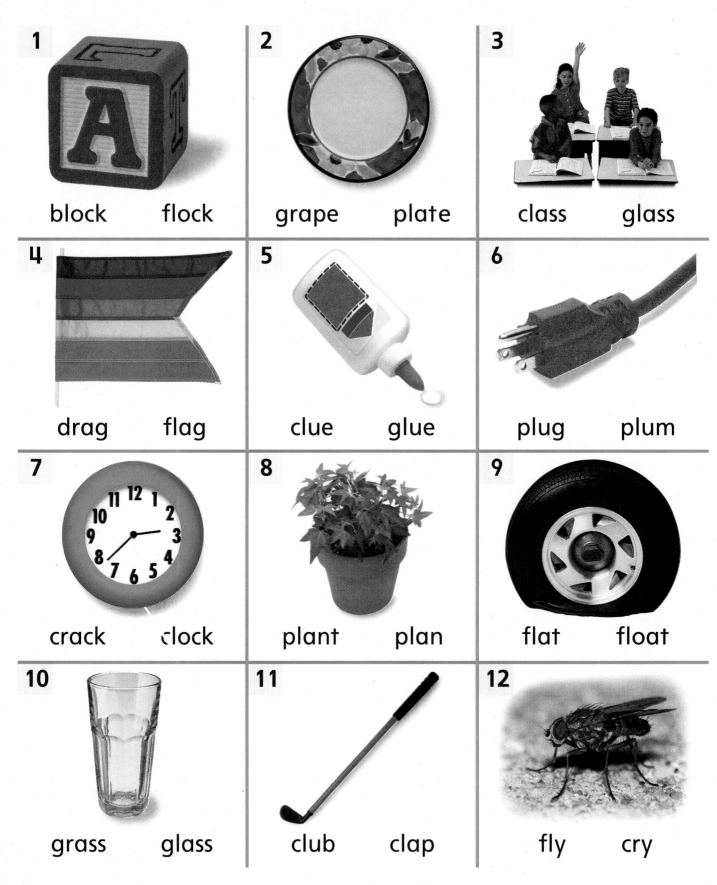

1 block   flock

2 grape   plate

3 class   glass

4 drag   flag

5 clue   glue

6 plug   plum

7 crack   clock

8 plant   plan

9 flat   float

10 grass   glass

11 club   clap

12 fly   cry

Lesson 118
L blends: Picture-text match

Home

Point to a picture and have your child name another word that has the same beginning sound.

Say the name of each picture. Print its beginning blend on the line. Trace the whole word.

1	2	3
club	ant	ag

4	5	6
ate	ock	y

7	8	9
at	ass	ock

10	11	12
obe	ug	ue

1.

Take a peek into my

_____

_____ .

clap
class
grass

2.

Tim draws a funny

_____

_____ .

clock
clown
frown

3.

Fran makes a clock from a paper

_____

_____ .

plate
prank
plum

4.

Mr. Glen lets us grow

_____

_____ .

plans
plates
plants

5.

We play with clay and

_____

_____ .

braids
drives
blocks

6.

We look at the

_____

_____ .

globe
glass
grape

 THINK! **Would you like to do what Tim and Fran did in school? Why?**

**Spice smells nice,
And tastes good, too.
But too much spice
Can spoil the stew.**

▶ Say the name of the first picture in the row. Circle each picture in the row whose name begins with the same blend.

1	swing				
2	spill				
3	skate				
4	sled				
5	snail				
6	stop				

Say the name of each picture. **Circle** its name.

1. sled   slide

2. stops   steps

3. spill   spade

4. skunk   spunk

5. spin   swim

6. scrap   scrub

7. sweet   street

8. smoke   spoke

9. square   scare

10. swing   string

11. snake   skate

12. spot   spoon

Home

Point to a picture and ask your child
to think of a word that rhymes.

Say the name of each picture. Print its beginning blend on the line. Trace the whole word.

1. skate

2. ed

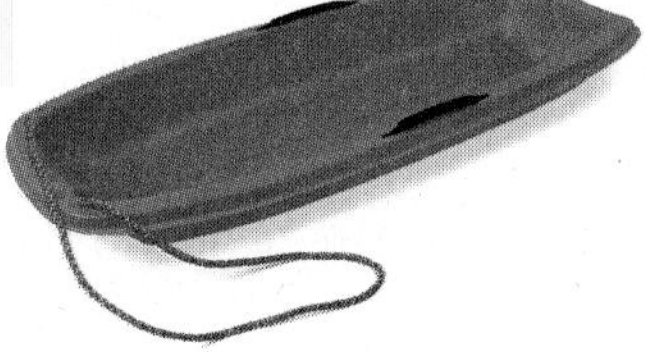

3. ub

4. ar

5. ail

6. op

7. oke

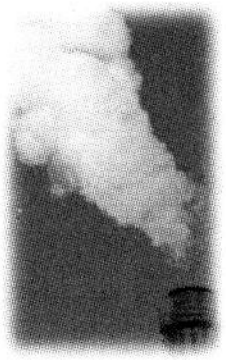

8. irt

9. ill

10. ing

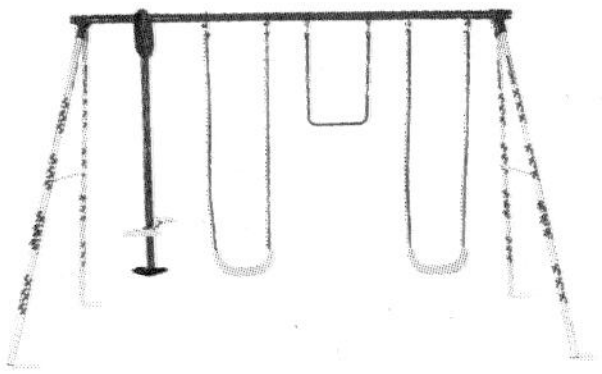

11. are

12. im

Say **the name of the picture.** Circle **the word that will finish the sentence.** Print **it on the line.**

1. Be sure to _____ and read the rules!

spill
stop
star

2. Take turns on the _____.

slide
sling
slip

3. Do not run near the _____.

sting
swing
swim

4. Please do not pet the _____.

snake
spoke
snail

5. Look before you cross the _____.

steps
street
stamp

6. Always _____ with a pal.

sweep
snake
swim

 THINK! What other safety rules do you know?

Lesson 121
S blends: Words in context

 **Home** Ask your child to read the sentences.

Jim wants milk. Sue needs rice.
Mom says some ice cream would be nice.

Get some paper. Make a list,
So that nothing will be missed.

> **Say** the name of the first picture in the row. **Circle** each picture in the row whose name ends with the same blend.

1 jump   

2 desk  

3 sink  

4 list    

5 swing    

Say the name of each picture. **Print** its ending blend on the line. **Trace** the whole word.

1

trunk

2

la_____

3

de_____

4

mi_____

5

li_____

6

wi_____

7

ne_____

8

si_____

9

ma_____

10

ri_____

11

ju_____

12

ki_____

Lesson 122
Final blends: Spelling

Home

Ask your child to point to a picture, spell the word, and name the letters in the final blend.

Blend the letter sounds together as you say each word. **Color** the picture it names.

1

sl e d

2

cr i b

3

pl u g

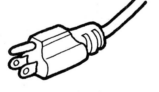  

4

fl a t

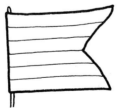  

5

dr u m

Blend the letter sounds together as you say each word. Then **print** the word on the line. **Draw** a line to the picture it names.

1

s i nk

————————

- - - - - - -

———————— ●

2

l i st

————————

- - - - - - -

———————— ●

3

m i lk

————————

- - - - - - -

———————— ●

4

r i ng

————————

- - - - - - -

———————— ●

5

j u mp

————————

- - - - - - -

———————— ●

6

d e sk

————————

- - - - - - -

———————— ●

Lesson 123
Final blends: Blending

Home

Read a word aloud and ask your child to name the final blend.

 **Phonics & Reading**

 Read the story. Then use words from the story to finish the sentences.

A Friend in Need

Champ had a cold in his chest.
Hank made a soft bed for Champ.
He gave him warm broth to drink.
He gave him good things to eat.

"Fresh food will help," said Hank.
"You will get well fast."

Champ gave Hank a great big kiss.

"Thank you, Champ," Hank said.
"You are my best friend!"

1. Hank gave Champ warm _____.

2. He gave Champ good _____ to eat.

3. Champ is Hank's _____ friend.

THINK! How can good food help you get well?

Lesson 124
Review consonant blends: Reading
257

Phonics & Writing

Write a get-well note to send to Champ. Try to cheer Champ up. The words below may help you.

rest	play	want	jump	bring
kind	think	fast	glad	friend

Dear Champ,

_____

_____

_____

_____

_____

_____

_____

_____

_____

_____

_____

Your friend,

_____

_____

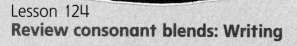

Ask your child to read the story on page 257 to you.

Won't you try my berry pie?
The crust is flaky, my, oh my.
Come on, have some.
Don't be shy.
If you won't try it, I may cry.

Say the name of the picture. Circle the words in the boxes with the same sound of **y** as the picture name. Circle the pictures whose names have the vowel sound of **y**.

1	by	lazy	yellow	dry	yet
	my	sky	yoke	cry	yarn
2	yes	fry	you	yard	funny
	yellow	puppy	sly	yell	windy
3	fly	candy	yams	lady	penny
20	pry	fairy	baby	try	pony

1

puppy   buggy

2

fry   fly

3

lady   baby

4

funny   penny

5

pony   penny

6

cry   try

7

spy   sky

8

fifty   twenty

9

sly   fry

 Home

Point to a picture and ask your child to think of a word that has the same beginning sound.

Say the name of each picture. **Circle** the word that will finish the sentence. **Print** it on the line.

1. Wendy can not ride a
   _____
   - - - - - - - - - - - - - - -
   _____.

   bony
   pony
   penny

2. She is too small to feed a
   _____
   - - - - - - - - - - - - - - -
   _____.

   puffy
   poppy
   puppy

3. She can't draw the
   _____
   - - - - - - - - - - - - - - -
   _____.

   sky
   sly
   spy

4. Mom will not let her eat
   _____
   - - - - - - - - - - - - - - -
   _____.

   sandy
   candy
   funny

5. I feel sad if she starts to
   _____
   - - - - - - - - - - - - - - -
   _____.

   my
   cry
   try

6. Wendy is just a tiny
   _____
   - - - - - - - - - - - - - - -
   _____.

   bunny
   baby
   buggy

 What can a tiny baby do?

Say the name of each picture. Print the picture
name on the line. In the last box, draw a picture
of a word in which **y** is a vowel. Write the word.

1

- - -

2

- - -

3

- - -

4

- - -

5

- - -

6

- - -

7

- - -

8

- - -

9

- - -

Lesson 126
Y as a vowel: Spelling

Home

Ask your child to say the picture
name and spell the word.

 **Phonics & Spelling**

▶ Read **the sentences. Use** the mixed-up letters to make a word. **Print** the word on the line to finish the sentence.

1. "The fruit looks _____," Clare said.

s h r e f

2. "Let's buy some _____," said Greg.

u p l m s

3. "I'll _____ to find ripe ones."

r t y

4. "Just _____ the grapes!" Clare said.

e l l s m

5. "Now all we need is _____."

e a d b r

6. "Milk is on our _____ too," Greg said.

i s l t

 **How do you think the grapes smell?**

Phonics & Writing

▶ **Write** a shopping list for your family's next trip to the store. **List** things to buy. **Look** at the words in the box for help.

bread	drink	sweet	fruit
things	grapes	milk	candy

SHOPPING LIST

Book Corner

Molly's Broccoli
by Deborah Eaton

Molly doesn't want to eat broccoli. Then she finds something good to mix it with.

Home Talk with your child about what items could be added to the list.

TALK ABOUT IT

What toppings would you like to spread on pizza?

8

PIZZA FEAST

This book belongs to:

1

Slice up good things. Try different kinds of toppings.

6

Press the dough in a pan. Make it flat and round.

3

FOLD

FOLD

To make pizza, first mix flour, water, and yeast. This makes dough.

2

Bake the pizza. Let the cheese melt. Let the crust get crisp. Mmmm. It smells great!

7

Spread sauce all over the dough.

4

Next, spread cheese over the sauce.

5

Say the name of each picture. **Fill in** the bubble beside the picture name.

1
- ○ trip
- ○ prize
- ○ train
- ○ drain

2
- ○ snail
- ○ snake
- ○ skate
- ○ string

3
- ○ clock
- ○ braid
- ○ blouse
- ○ block

4
- ○ crab
- ○ grab
- ○ club
- ○ crib

5
- ○ flag
- ○ glass
- ○ flat
- ○ black

6
- ○ green
- ○ dress
- ○ drum
- ○ desk

7
- ○ swim
- ○ sting
- ○ swing
- ○ sweet

8
- ○ clap
- ○ plant
- ○ plug
- ○ plate

9
- ○ stamp
- ○ steps
- ○ stop
- ○ spill

10
- ○ glue
- ○ globe
- ○ drive
- ○ glove

11
- ○ frame
- ○ lamp
- ○ fly
- ○ frog

12
- ○ glass
- ○ spot
- ○ spoon
- ○ smoke

▶ **Circle** the word that will finish each sentence. **Print** it on the line.

1. _____ the day with a good meal.

Stop
Start
Star

2. Corn _____ and milk are great.

flags
frames
flakes

3. _____ adding some fruit.

Fry
Try
Why

4. _____ a glass of juice, too.

Drink
Trunk
Dress

5. Eat only good _____.

rings
swings
things

6. Stay away from _____ things.

sweet
smoke
square

Sing Along

Rain, Rain, Rain, and Wind

Rain, rain, rain and wind,
What a stormy day!
When the sun comes out again,
We'll go out and play.

▶ **Name some things children like
to do inside in rainy weather.**

THINK! **Do you like to go out on a
stormy day? Why or why not?**

Unit 5
Introduction
269

Home Letter

Dear Family,

Your child will want to tell you about what we'll be doing in the next few weeks—learning to read and write contractions and words ending with ed and ing. We'll also learn about words that begin with consonant digraphs. A consonant digraph is formed with two letters that stand for one sound, such as the following.

th  **wh**  **sh**  **ch**  **kn**

thermometer   **whistle**   **sheep**   **chimney**   **knot**

The theme for this unit will be something that affects all of us everyday—the weather!

At-Home Activities

Here are some activities you and your child might like to do together.

▶ Spend a few minutes listening to a weather forecast with your child. The next day, have your child draw a picture of the weather that actually occurred. If a thermometer is available, help your child read the temperature and record it under the drawing. Talk about differences between the weather forecast and the actual weather.

▶ Explore how a change in the weather affects what we wear and what we do.

Book Corner

You and your child might enjoy reading these books together.

Weather Everywhere
by Denise Casey
Common questions about weather are answered simply and clearly.

A Snow Story
by Melvin J. Leavitt
Johnny explores the lake and the forest after a giant snowstorm.

Sincerely,

It has rained and poured all week.
And now it's raining again.
The puddles are getting so big!
I'm jumping and hopping in them.

> **Say** the name of each picture. **Print** the ending you see in the corner of the box to finish its name. **Trace** the whole word.

1 ed

spilled

2 ed

melt

3 ing

eat

4 ing

rain

5 ed

mail

6 ing

fish

7 ed

row

8 ed

peel

9 ing

cry

Read the word below each picture. Each picture name has a base word and an ending. **Read** the words beside each picture. Each word ends with the same sound as the picture name. **Circle** each base word.

#	Picture				
1	jump(ed)	asked	yelled	fixed	played
		mixed	rocked	bumped	rained
2	rea(d)ing	going	telling	sailing	mixing
		asking	waiting	resting	boating
3	mel(t)ed	waited	seated	heated	landed
		mailed	loaded	floated	ended
4	coo(k)ing	rowing	crying	flying	fishing
		picking	saying	eating	melting

Lesson 130
Inflectional endings -ed and -ing

 With your child, hunt for words with endings in favorite storybooks.

**Circle the word that will finish the sentence.
Print it on the line.**

1

_____

We were _____ to eat.

waiting
waited

2

_____

Dad was _____ the ham.

cooking
cooked

3

_____

Mom _____ us to help, too.

asking
asked

4

_____

She was _____ the baby.

dressing
dressed

5

_____

Sandy _____ the fruit.

peeling
peeled

6

_____

I _____ the eggs and toast.

fixing
fixed

THINK!

**How does this family
help each other?**

Lesson 131
Inflectional endings -ed and -ing

273

Circle the word that will finish the sentence.
Print it on the line.

1

_____

Dad was _____ fishing.

go

going

2

_____

I _____ him to take me
to Mary's home.

asking

asked

3

_____

We were _____ a ball
to each other.

kicked

kicking

4

_____

Then we _____ to get wet.

started

starting

5

_____

It was _____ cats and dogs.

rain

raining

6

_____

We _____ for the rain
to stop.

waiting

waited

7

_____

Then we _____ on Mary's
swing set.

played

playing

THINK! **What does "raining cats and dogs" mean?**

Lesson 131
Inflectional endings -ed and -ing

 Using words with endings, take turns
telling what you did today.

My soft mittens are thick not thin.
My fingers and thumbs stay warm in them.
When the thermometer says thirty-three,
Outside with my mittens is where I'll be.

> **Thumb** begins with the sound of **th**. Circle each picture whose name begins with the sound of **th**.

1	2	3	4
👍	3	2	tiger

5	6	7	8
rose	girl thinking	30	thermometer

9	10	11	12
train	thread spool	tie	13

1
thick

2
in

3
ire

4
ink

5
irty

6
ie

7
iger

8
ape

9
ree

10
umb

11
orn

12
en

Lesson 132
Discriminating between th and t

Ask your child to read each picture name.

The wind whips and whistles.
It whips through the tree.
It whirls around my window.
And takes my white cap from me!

White **begins with the sound of wh.** Circle **each
picture whose name begins with the sound of wh.**

1

_____ eel

2

_____ umb

3

_____ ick

4

_____ orn

5

_____ eat

6

_____ ink

7

_____ ale

8

_____ in

9

_____ ite

10

_____ ree

11

_____ read

12

_____ istle

 Ask your child: What comes after two and before four? Take turns making up riddles for other picture names.

Sharon is in the sunlight.
And what does she see?
A shiny, shimmering shadow.
She says, "You can't catch me!"

> Shadow **begins with the sound of sh.** Circle each picture whose name begins with the sound of **sh.**

1

2

3

4

5

6

7

8

9

10

11

12

Say the name of each picture. **Print sh or s** to finish each word. **Trace** the whole word.

1 ___ ell

2 ___ ail

3 ___ ade

4 ___ ix

5 ___ oe

6 ___ elf

7 ___ ip

8 ___ eep

9 ___ eat

10 ___ irt

11 ___ ock

12 ___ out

Lesson 134
Discriminating between sh and s: Spelling

 Ask your child to make sentences using some of the words.

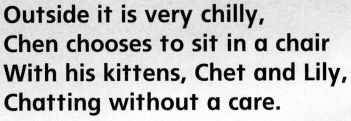

Outside it is very chilly,
Chen chooses to sit in a chair
With his kittens, Chet and Lily,
Chatting without a care.

▶ **Chair** begins with the sound of **ch**. Circle each
picture whose name begins with the sound of **ch**.

1

2

3

4

5

6

7

8

9

10

11

12

Say the name of each picture. Print ch or c to finish each word. Trace the whole word.

1 in	**2** eck	**3** oat
4 eese	**5** ube	**6** ick
7 alk	**8** ave	**9** ain
10 erry	**11** ow	**12** air

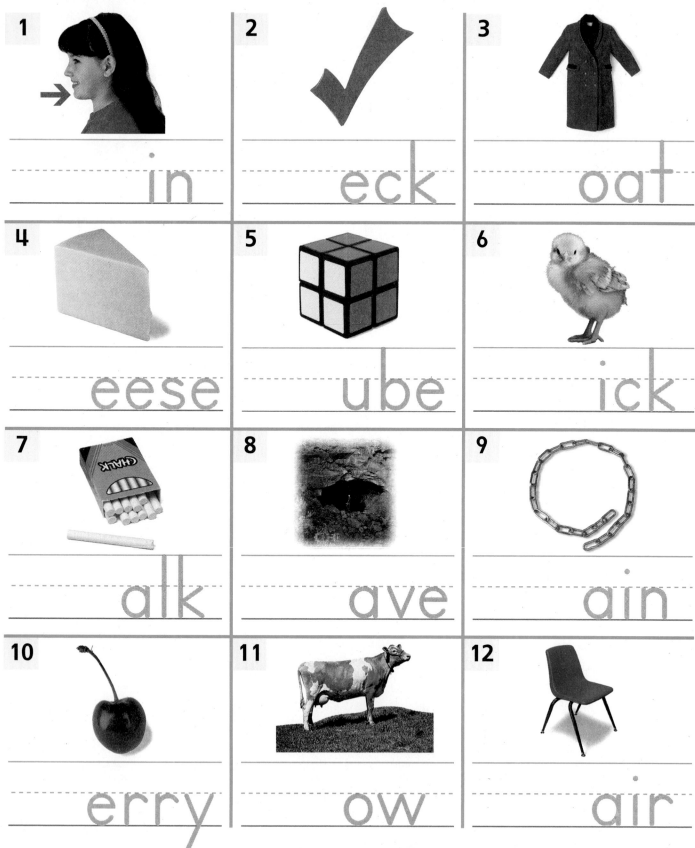

282

Lesson 135
Ch and c: Spelling

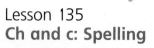

Ask your child to identify common household items whose names begin with *ch* or *c*.

Knock, knock, knock.
Who's knocking at the door?
We know who it is—
The wind, and nothing more!

Knock begins with the letters **kn.** You only hear the sound of **n.** Say the name of each picture. Circle the letters that stand for the beginning sound. Circle the pictures whose names begin with **kn.**

1	2	3
knee	think	knot

4	5	6
knob	knife	whale

7	8	9
chin	knock	knit

Circle the sentence that tells about the picture.

1.

    The tire is black and white.

    Chad tied a knot in the rope.

2.

    Randy did not skin his knee.

    Kelly kneels down on the mat.

3.

    Did you hear a knock at the door?

    Did Nick knock over the vase?

4.

    I fed the bread to the chicks.

    I used a knife to slice the cheese.

5.

    Chuck knows where his watch is.

    Kate turned the knob to the left.

6.

    Susan knits a sweater for her sister.

    Jenny ties a knot with her shoe strings.

7.

    The knight does not ride a horse.

    The knight rides a horse with spots.

Lesson 136
Consonant digraph kn

Home Ask your child to point to and read each *kn* word.

Circle **the word that will finish the sentence.**
Print **it on the line.**

1

_____

_ _ _ _ _ _ _ _ _ _ _ _ _

Chuck _____ about a sunny beach.

knows
knob
knock

2

_____

_ _ _ _ _ _ _ _ _ _ _ _ _

We catch the bus at _____.

thick
three
thorn

3

_____

_ _ _ _ _ _ _ _ _ _ _ _ _

Beth lays a _____ sheet in the shade.

white
wheat
whip

4

_____

_ _ _ _ _ _ _ _ _ _ _ _ _

Chuck fills his shoes with sea _____.

sheets
shades
shells

5

_____

_ _ _ _ _ _ _ _ _ _ _ _ _

I _____ Beth a new game.

teach
reach
cheat

6

_____

_ _ _ _ _ _ _ _ _ _ _ _ _

Then we sit and watch the _____.

shape
ships
shake

**What else might Chuck
and Beth do at the beach?**

Lesson 137
Review: Consonant digraphs

285

Read each clue. Print the answer to each riddle on the line. Use the cloud pictures if you need help.

three	sheep	wheel	cherry
ship	chick	whale	knife

1. My hair is called wool.
   I can be white, brown, or black.

   _____

   I am a _____.

2. I hatch out of an egg.
   My mother is a hen.

   _____

   I am a _____.

3. I live in the sea.
   I am much bigger than a fish.

   _____

   I am a _____.

4. I sail across the sea.
   People ride in me.

   _____

   I am a _____.

5. I come after two
   and before four.

   _____

   I am _____.

6. I am round. I help
   cars and bikes go.

   _____

   I am a _____.

7. I am round and red.
   I am good to eat.

   _____

   I am a _____.

8. I am very sharp.
   Use me to cut things.

   _____

   I am a _____.

Lesson 137
Review consonant digraphs

Home

Ask your child to read the riddles to you so you can guess the answers.

Blend the letter sounds together as you say the word. Print the word on the line. Draw a line to the picture it names.

1 ch i n

→ _____

●

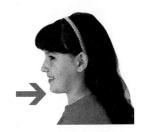

2 th i n k

→ _____

●

3 kn o b

→ _____

●

4 sh e l f

→ _____

●

5 wh e a t

→ _____

●

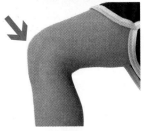

6 kn e e

→ _____

●

Look at the picture. Then follow the directions.

1. Color the ship black.
2. Circle the shell on the beach.
3. Write a three on the flag.
4. Color the wheel brown.
5. Color the thick rope yellow.
6. Draw a whale in the water.
7. Draw a box around the knot.
8. Color the sky blue but keep the cloud white.

Lesson 138
Review consonant digraphs

Home

With your child, make up a story to go with the picture.

▶ **Read** the story. **Use** words in which two letters stand for one beginning sound and words with endings to finish the sentences.

Thump and Chomp

Sheri walked home from school in the rain.
This is what she heard.
THUMP and CHOMP.
THUMP and CHOMP.
What could it be?

"I think I know," said Sheri.
She turned the knob on the door.
There was Chester all wet and all muddy.
Chester's tail was thumping.
Chester's mouth was chomping.

_____

1. Sheri _____ home in the rain.

2. She turned the _____ on the door.

3. Chester's tail was _____.

4. His mouth was _____.

Why do you think Chester was all wet and all muddy?

Phonics & Writing

Write about something funny that happened to you. The words in the box may help you.

know	think	thumping
when	chill	opened

Lesson 139
Review endings, digraphs, contractions: Writing

Home Ask your child to read the story to you.

What kind of weather would each kind of cloud bring?

8

Cumulonimbus clouds

6

Clouds that bring thunder almost touch the ground. Their tops reach high into the sky.

FOLD

FOLD

CLOUDS

This book belongs to:

Cirrus clouds

3

These thin, curly clouds are called mare's tails. Do you know why?

1

7

When clouds change, the weather may change, too!

5

Fair-weather clouds are fluffy and white. Their shapes keep changing.

Cumulus clouds

FOLD

FOLD

Clouds come in many shapes, sizes, and colors.

2

It may be raining when you see low clouds like a heavy, gray sheet.

Stratus clouds

4

Lesson 140
Review endings, consonant digraphs: Take-Home Book

They'll slide down
They will go very fast.
I'll slide, too.
But I will be last.

I will = I'll
he will = he'll

you will = you'll
she will = she'll
it will = it'll

they will = they'll
we will = we'll

▶ **They'll** is a short way to say **they will**. Read each sentence. Circle the short way to write the underlined words.

1	It will be fun to go for a ride on a sled.	You'll It'll
2	I will get on the sled.	We'll I'll
3	You will get on the sled with me.	You'll She'll
4	They will all get on the sled, too.	They'll It'll
5	Oh, no! Get off or we will fall!	he'll we'll

 Why might the children fall off the sled?

she is = she's   it is = it's   he is = he's

1 <u>It is</u> a nice day to play in the park.

_____ a nice day to play in the park.

2 <u>He is</u> going down the slide.

_____ going down the slide.

3 <u>She is</u> floating in the pool.

_____ floating in the pool.

4 <u>He is</u> playing on the swings.

_____ playing on the swings.

5 <u>It is</u> full of things to do!

_____ full of things to do!

THINK! What else can you do at the park?

Home Ask your child what words form the contractions *they'll*, *we'll*, and *you'll*.

I'm is a short way to say **I am**. Look at each picture.
Read the sentence. Print the short way to write the
underlined words. Use the words in the box to help you.

> I am = I'm   we are = we're
>
> you are = you're   they are = they're

1

I am going to the zoo with you.

_____

_ _ _ _ _ _ _ _ _ _ _ _ _ _ _ _ _

_____ going to the zoo with you.

2

We are going to ride the bus.

_____

_ _ _ _ _ _ _ _ _ _ _ _ _ _ _ _ _

_____ going to ride the bus.

3

You are going to see the seals.

_____

_ _ _ _ _ _ _ _ _ _ _ _ _ _ _ _ _

_____ going to see the seals.

4

They are going to see the cubs.

_____

_ _ _ _ _ _ _ _ _ _ _ _ _ _ _ _ _

_____ going to see the cubs.

5

I think we are going to like the zoo!

_____

_ _ _ _ _ _ _ _ _ _ _ _ _ _ _ _ _

I think _____ going to like the zoo!

**What other animals can
you see at the zoo?**

Can't is a short way to say **can not**. Read the sentences. Circle the short way to write the <u>underlined words</u>. Use the words in the box to help you.

| can not = can't | does not = doesn't |
| will not = won't | is not = isn't |

1
Wags <u>is not</u> clean.
He is a muddy mess!

can't
doesn't
isn't

2
Mom says he needs a bath.
Wags just <u>will not</u> get into the tub.

won't
isn't
doesn't

3
Wags <u>does not</u> like baths.
He runs away.

isn't
can't
doesn't

4
I <u>can not</u> catch him.
Mom will help me.

can't
doesn't
won't

5
Wags <u>is not</u> a muddy puppy now.
I am the one who needs a bath!

isn't
can't
doesn't

THINK! Who needs a bath now and why?

Lesson 142
Contractions with not

 Using the contractions, take turns making up other sentences about Wags.

► **Circle the sentence that tells about the picture.**

1
I'll eat the hot dog.
I'm going to read the book.

2
It's in the bag.
She'll sleep in the tent.

3
We won't go on the ride.
We're on the ride.

4
She's going to play on the swing.
They're going to like my painting.

5
You're going to rake the yard.
We'll drive up to the lake.

6
I can't skate very well on the ice.
He doesn't like ice cream on his cake.

Fill in the bubble beside the sentence that tells about the picture.

1
- ○ It's a dog.
- ○ It can't be a dog.
- ○ They're dogs.

2
- ○ He's on a bike.
- ○ She's in a jet.
- ○ I'm on the bus.

3
- ○ It won't rain today.
- ○ It'll rain all day.
- ○ I'll play in the rain.

4
- ○ We don't like bugs.
- ○ She'll eat a hot dog.
- ○ We're eating the fruit.

5
- ○ They'll go for a ride.
- ○ We'll go for a swim.
- ○ You're up a tree.

6
- ○ She can't find her shoes.
- ○ He doesn't want to ride his bike.
- ○ She's trying to catch a fish.

 Home

Ask your child to use contractions to tell about himself or herself.

Phonics & Spelling

Say and spell the words below. Print the words on the lines where they belong.

Word List

fishing   think

can't   melted   I'm   peeled   ship

knot   chin   whale   rowing   ship   spilled

Words that have **ed** endings.

1. _____   2. _____   3. _____

Words that take the place of two small words.

4. _____   5. _____

Words whose beginning sound is made up of two letters.

6. _____   7. _____   8. _____

9. _____   10. _____

Words that have **-ing** endings.

11. _____   12. _____

Phonics & Writing

What is your favorite kind of weather? What do you like to do outdoors? Write about it on the lines. Use some of your spelling words.

ship	you're	fishing	rowing
melted	whale	think	can't

Book Corner

A Rainbow Somewhere
by Nancy Dowd

On a rainy day, Jenny waits and waits to see a rainbow.

Review endings, digraphs, contractions: Writing

Ask your child to forecast tomorrow's weather.

6

"But I know it's raining," Chet said.
Trish opened the door and looked.

8

TALK ABOUT IT

What do you like to do
when it's raining?
What do you like to do
when it is sunny?

FOLD

FOLD

Chet and Trish looked out.
"It's raining," Trish said.
"We can't play out there."

3

IT'S RAINING

This book belongs to:

_____

1

"It isn't raining!" said Trish.
"It's Dad! He's making it rain!"

7

Mom looked out with them.
"See, it isn't raining," she told them.

5

FOLD   FOLD

"I'm working," said Mom.
"I can't play with you.
Why don't you go out?"

2

"We can't go out there,"
Chet said to Mom.
"It's raining."

4

Lesson 145
Review endings, digraphs, contractions: Take-Home Book

Say the name of each picture. Fill in the bubble beside the picture name.

1

○ knee
○ knob
○ knife

2

○ wheel
○ whip
○ white

3

○ chain
○ thin
○ chin

4

○ sheep
○ ship
○ chip

5

○ thin
○ cherry
○ three

6

○ knit
○ knot
○ knock

7

○ chair
○ shame
○ chat

8

○ while
○ throat
○ whale

9

○ throne
○ thumb
○ shade

Look at the picture. Circle the word that will finish the sentence. Print it on the line.

1

How deep do you _____ it is?

think
knew
chase

2

She's _____ to find out.

rowing
spilled
trying

3

It's up to his _____!

knot
chin
whale

4

She _____ get it out.

isn't
don't
can't

5

_____ happy that it snowed.

They're
I'll
It's

6

The snow has all _____!

peeled
spilled
melted

Lesson 146
Review endings, consonant digraphs, contractions: Unit Checkup